Praise for Laura June's *Now My Heart Is Full*

* * *

"This beautiful, heart-rending and -restoring memoir explores what it means to be a mother and a daughter, and coming to terms with the imperfections within these most foundational of familial bonds. Laura June writes with grace, wit, and honesty."
—*Nylon*

"Sometimes, a book swells into something far lovelier than you assume it will be. Laura June's warm and moving *Now My Heart Is Full* is one such unforgettable book. What seems like a straightforward memoir about motherhood slowly, carefully, becomes so much more. This is the story of how the daughter of an alcoholic mother becomes a motherless mother and reconciles the ways she was loved, the ways she was hurt, and how the birth of her own daughter allowed her heart to finally grow full. There is no maudlin sentimentality here. Instead, Laura June writes with wit and melancholy, unabashed joy and tenderness. Imagine my surprise, when I reached the end, and found myself in tears."
—Roxane Gay, *New York Times* bestselling author of *Hunger*

"Is there any more formative bond than the one between mother and daughter? Laura June's heartbreaking but ultimately hopeful memoir intertwines the story of her daughter's birth with an insightful and forgiving account of her own mother's alcoholism and their complex relationship. A moving, beautiful exploration of what it means to love—and let go."
—Julie Buntin, author of *Marlena*

"Laura June's writing is affecting, clear-eyed, and honest. Her ambivalence toward many of life's biggest milestones is particularly refreshing in a culture that demands a woman's every attention be paid to marriage and motherhood. But *Now My Heart Is Full* is not cynical, or cutting—rather, it is surprised by its own warmth and joy."

—Katie Heaney, author of *Never Have I Ever*

"*Now My Heart Is Full* explores in heartfelt prose how the familial ties that bond us are inevitably the ones that threaten to break us—and the messy miracle of breaking them first. Laura June triumphs by resisting the inertia of inherited suffering and surrendering to the possibility of a boundless, unbreakable love."

—Alana Massey, author of *All the Lives I Want*

PENGUIN BOOKS

NOW MY HEART IS FULL

Laura June was born and raised in Pittsburgh, Pennsylvania. Her writing has appeared on *The Awl, BuzzFeed, Jezebel,* and *The Outline,* and in *New York Magazine, Cosmopolitan,* and *The Washington Post*. She was previously a staff writer at *New York Magazine's The Cut,* and is a contributing writer at *The Outline*.

NOW MY HEART IS FULL

A MEMOIR

· · ·

LAURA JUNE

PENGUIN BOOKS

PENGUIN BOOKS

An imprint of Penguin Random House LLC
375 Hudson Street
New York, New York 10014
penguin.com

Portions of Chapter 6 first appeared in different form on *The Awl* as
"Other People's Babies" in 2014 and "No Offense to Laura Ingalls Wilder"
in 2015. Portions of Chapter 20 first appeared in different form on *The Cut*
(a website of *New York Magazine*) as "Having a Daughter Helped Me
Understand My Own Mother" in 2015.

LIBRARY OF CONGRESS CATALOGING-IN-PUBLICATION DATA

Names: June, Laura, author.
Title: Now my heart is full: a memoir / Laura June.
Description: New York, New York : Penguin Books, an imprint of
Penguin Random House LLC, 2018.
Identifiers: LCCN 2017042062 (print) I LCCN 2018016487 (ebook) I ISBN
9781524704698 (ebook) I ISBN 9780143130918 I ISBN 9780143130918
(paperback) I
ISBN 0143130919(paperback) I ISBN 9781524704698(ebook) I ISBN
1524704695(ebook)
Subjects: LCSH: Motherhood. I Mothers and daughters. I June, Laura—Family. I
Autobiography. I LCGFT: Autobiographies.
Classification: LCC HQ759 (ebook) I LCC HQ759 .J85 2018 (print) I DDC
306.874/3—dc23
LC record available at https://lccn.loc.gov/2017042062

Printed in the United States of America
1   3   5   7   9   10   8   6   4   2

Set in Berling LT Std   •   Designed by Elke Sigal

For Zelda June Topolsky,
Who insisted I use her full name.

And for Josh,
Who insisted.

No more sadness, I kiss it good-bye
The sun is bursting right out of the sky
I searched the whole world for someone like you
    —MADONNA, "TRUE BLUE," 1986

NOW
MY HEART
IS FULL

• • •

CHAPTER 1

. . .

On a Tuesday in February of 2014, at 1:45 p.m., at the age of thirty-six, I became a mother for the first time, and my daughter became my daughter.

We named her Zelda June. She was born via Cacsarean section in a scheduled, quick, and largely drama-free operation that lasted roughly a half hour from start to finish. I wouldn't exactly say it was "painless," but it was close enough to painless that I still have trouble telling other women who have had children about the experience for fear that I will sound as though I'm bragging. "She has a high tolerance for pain," my husband, Josh, has interjected when I mention my easy recovery. As I sit here now, I can barely feel the scar she left on me. It is barely visible when I look at my body in the mirror.

Those moments there, when Zelda became Zelda and I became her mother, they washed away decades of ambivalence and fear, of random nightmares or missed opportunities and chances walked away from. Washed away were the babies I hadn't had, in the face of the one I did.

I was, like I said, thirty-six years old. I'd been married for almost seven years and had lived in New York City for nine. I put off the pregnancy for as long as I could, telling myself I was too busy; there would be time later. But later was always later, and really, I was afraid; physically, emotionally, mentally, I feared pregnancy and motherhood. I didn't think too hard about it, and every six months or a year, Josh randomly brought it up and then just as quickly let it pass.

"Should we have a baby, Laura?" I'd hear from the other room.

"What do you want for dinner?" I'd ask, changing the subject. We'd talked about kids when we got engaged, when we got married: yes, I'd say. I'd like to have kids someday. Someday was off in the future. Someday, I could handle. But someday was stretched out for years as I put it off, put it off.

But then, in the middle of 2013, I changed my mind. Someday arrived.

I could tell you I had a change of heart, and I did. I could tell you that I was finally comfortable enough, finally felt financially stable enough, owned a house that had a spare bedroom; all of these things took years to fall into place. But really, I was also rather suddenly overcome with an everyday, very common desire: I wanted to be a mother, and I knew that it might take a while to become pregnant. At thirty-five, I thought, "Well, better start trying, I guess."

And then I got pregnant almost immediately.

I confirmed my pregnancy with a test on my thirty-sixth birthday, and as I stood in the bathroom, with only a few moments before I opened the door and told my husband, I cried silently in the dark into a towel. I had only just decided, less than a month ago, that I wanted to have a baby, and now there I was, the wheels set in motion: the first step had been a success! I was pregnant. But still, I cried tears of cowardice, of anxiety, and of simple disbelief. Telling Josh, I knew, would set off the chain of events that would end in . . . well, the birth of a baby. I closed my eyes and breathed really deep. I reached behind me and hit the light switch. The bathroom was small, in the center of the second floor of our tiny (it was just eleven and a half feet wide) Brooklyn townhouse. I loved that bathroom, its claw-footed tub, but also the fact that it had no windows. When you turned off the light, you were in total darkness and quiet. It was the only place in the house where that was possible. I screamed into a towel. I didn't know how to feel. I'd spent so long avoiding even thinking about if I wanted to have children, and then, after years of doing the same thing, I stopped. We decided: "Yes," I said. "I think we should have a baby."

We had made every major decision that way: I said no by avoiding saying anything, until I said yes. It is in this way that I am, I guess, in control: I hold the Yes cards.

Change has always been hard for me, and though I moved through this phase—the pregnant-but-in-denial stage—very quickly, in just a few days, I'd be lying if I pretended it didn't happen.

One of the things that had occurred in the course of our marriage was that, like I said, every so often, Josh had brought up the possibility of having children. He said this—"Should we have a baby?"—as easily as if he were asking if I thought we should get a new couch or some other major but not life-altering purchase. For him, it wasn't much different than leasing a car, really: changes, even big ones, come fast and easy to him. This offsets, to some degree, me, to whom change comes neither easily nor quickly.

"Easy for you to say," I'd respond, and I was perfectly correct—it *was* easy for him to say—and then I'd go about throwing up all the potential roadblocks I could think of, simply to defer having to even think about the question. I'd have to have the fucking kid. He would just be the . . . dad. It wasn't him resigning his body to whatever it was that pregnancy entailed.

It went on this way for years, and for a really big chunk of that, I had the best excuse one could think of for deferring having a child: our apartment was too small. Of course, this was New York City, and our apartment was probably eight hundred square feet—which was massive compared to many people, plenty of whom had kids—but the argument did sort of, at least, hold water with Josh. I worried too, of course, about money, and that argument was also pretty valid. Brooklyn is very expensive, and for the first years of our marriage, we simply didn't have the financial stability that seemed completely reasonable to expect before having a baby.

So we just avoided *really* talking about a child—even a theoretical, future one—for a very long time.

But here's how an argument—whether a loud and angry one, a strategic one, or even a meaningless one about a trivial point; it doesn't matter—goes between Josh and me: He votes for change; I vote against it. He's progressive; I'm conservative.

I wish this weren't the case, but like I said, decisions, even big ones, are fairly effortless for him. He's "not guided by fear," he likes to say. I don't think of myself as fearful, just cautious, and caution is easily mistaken for fear, because it often results in inaction. Having a routine, things being stable and pre-dictable, is very necessary for me to be able to function, so I sometimes view major changes with suspicion at the start. It's not that I have a particularly troublesome time actually making decisions; it's just that I often draw out the period before. For a long time, I put off having the conversation. I'm not proud of this, but it is what comes naturally to me. I've been trying to change over the past decade, because I know how paralyzing and irritating it can be.

This was how we bought our house. Josh had wanted to buy a house or apartment for years before we'd even had the money. Dreaming big, even when it's not realistic in any way, has always kind of been his thing.

I didn't want to move. I loved our apartment, and I couldn't imagine a better one, only a worse one, with less light or lower ceilings. We had a huge, beautiful loft—how could we ever replace it? It was the same with the baby. I couldn't imagine a baby, and if I did, I thought usually only of the negatives: a loss of freedom and mental space, all the work I assumed a baby would be. I didn't imagine its beauty or how a child would add to my life. Josh imagined the best-case scenario, while I fantasized about the worst one.

But once enough years passed, and suddenly we *did* have the money to maybe buy a house, I remained steadfastly opposed to it conceptually, simply out of a resistance to change, even as I relented and walked up the streets of our neighborhood, checking out houses and apartments for sale. "You're humoring me," Josh used to say, but that wasn't exactly it. I was simply waiting for the right moment. And when the right house, built in 1863, on a shady and quiet street, appeared in our sights, I knew in just a few minutes: it should be ours, if it could be.

I never know what I'm going to order at a restaurant until I do it. I didn't know I wanted a baby until I did.

I was wrong about owning a house; it was awesome. And I was incredibly wrong about the baby: she is the best, most challenging, and most rewarding thing to have ever happened to us, and to me.

◆　◆　◆

In the days since my daughter's birth, I have felt on many occasions what I can only describe as "privileged" to know her, so clear it is to me that she's not my property. She's not mine, but her own being, and has been from day one on this planet. But I've never felt it more clearly than I did in that first moment, when we were literally separate for the first time, after ten months, and I saw clearly, only for a minute, the road ahead.

We'd been two people living together, Josh and I, for a long time. Then there had been an odd, somewhat lonely period of limbo in my pregnancy: I had the possibility of another person inside me, but she wasn't something I could *really* share yet, not even with Josh. Her existence seemed reliant wholly on me. And now, here we were. I knew what lay ahead: we were fucked, maybe. I was as unprepared for motherhood, I thought, as a person could be. I hadn't been around a baby in years, didn't know what having one would be like. This inability to imagine what life would look like on the other side, when the baby arrived, troubled me.

But for a moment, everything was perfect. Zelda asserted herself with her howling, angry bawling, Josh was in tears and silent for once, and I was simply there. Her arrival silenced me. Everything had changed, but I had no idea how yet. I was simply her mother.

And in that moment of my daughter's birth, just Josh and

me (and all the doctors and nurses) there to witness it, I thought of my own mother. My mother, who had been dead for seven years. My mother, who had loved me and had been beautiful and caring and intelligent. My mother, who had had four babies before she was thirty. My mother, who also had been an alcoholic, whose body simply gave up on life when she was fifty-four years old. My mother, who I walked away from at the age of eighteen and with whom I never really had a relationship worth mentioning again. My mother, Kathy, who was complicated and painful for me to think about still, even though she had been gone for almost a decade. It was my mother I thought of as I looked down at my new daughter, this child I'd never been sure I wanted until the moment I knew that I was pregnant.

I didn't say it aloud that day. I didn't say to Josh or to Zelda, "I wish my mother was here." I knew that Josh knew this; it hung heavily in the air. The happiness of those moments was countered only by her, my mother, and her absence. I didn't say it out loud, but I felt it keenly and was taken aback by the feeling. In hindsight, it's not surprising, but at the time, I was shocked by my childlike wish to have my mother there, to wish her back from the dead, to have a time machine to change the past, to erase terrible things I'd said to her and terrible things she'd done to me. I wanted in those few minutes, when Zelda's body was new and still covered in the evidence of her birth, to crawl backward and change almost everything about my relationship with my mother. To pave over what had actually happened with something more meaningful and less terribly sad. I imagined myself into the future, where I'd begin to tell Zelda about my mother, her grandmother, and was overwhelmed. What would I tell her? Would I lie? Would I say she'd been a wonderful woman who would have loved her and nurtured her the way she had loved and nurtured my brothers and me? Or would I tell her my mother was sick and lonely and mysterious and sometimes so like a black hole that even her adoring children couldn't get inside of her? Was there some space between a fake, fairy-tale version and an unvarnished truth?

In the moments of Zelda's birth, I saw the world with eyes that were open and accepting. That's why I wanted my mother: even if she remained unchanged, I'd introduce her, drunk and slurring, to my newborn baby. In all my imagined versions of my life, I'd never pictured that to be true; in fact, I would have died to stand in the way of letting her at her worst into my daughter's life, to let her find new ways of disappointing me, but in those few minutes, I was clear and, I imagined, had an approach to the world approximating what I've always thought monks or nuns must have. Accepting. Peace-filled. Full of an unfettered ability to love everyone equally. Even as it was happening, I knew this moment wouldn't last. But for just a little bit, I had a window into something my cynical, self-protecting mind rarely had access to.

It wouldn't be accurate to say I then felt regret for the way my relationship with my mother had unfolded, but it was true then that I did see other ways it could have. Other ways I could have been, and wanted to be, moving forward. And that afternoon the seeds were planted that I could probably, after years of telling myself the same story of my own life, and the story of my mother, tell another one. I saw that there might be another version, another way of thinking about it, a way that was truer than what I had previously told myself. After decades of believing that "making peace" with something consisted largely of saying, "Fuck it, we did our best," I saw the possibility of something more nuanced.

I had always thought that when people die, our relationships with them stop evolving. But I realized then that this wasn't true.

From the moment my daughter was born and my relationship with her began, I have felt an overwhelming awareness of my own place in time to my mother that exists both in the past and in the now. I am able to think differently about my relationship with her, as she's become not just my mother but also Zelda's grandmother. My grandmother is Margaret June, my mother is Kathleen June, and I am Laura June. When we named Zelda, Zelda, we also named her June. Zelda June. Another girl joining a long line of women with the middle name June. As part of me, as part of my mother and my grandmother, and going back in time further, to women I've never known or heard anything about.

The story of Zelda's birth is the most important one I have to tell. But first, before I tell you about how I decided to have a baby, I want to tell you about when I decided not to.

❖   ❖   ❖

My mother took me to have an abortion on Mother's Day in May of 1995. I was a senior in high school, and although I was not promiscuous by my own definition of the word, I wasn't 100 percent certain who the father of the baby was. I didn't have a boyfriend, really, and the boys I hung around with all fit a general profile: mostly a couple of years older than me, mostly dealing with their own shit. My life was about as confusing as it had ever been, and that confusion had only increased in the roughly two weeks since I'd found out I was pregnant, in the bathroom of my best friend Emily's mom's house, in the suburbs of Pittsburgh, where I had lived for most of my life.

It was almost certainly a Wednesday afternoon when I found out that I was pregnant, because Emily's mom worked late on Wednesdays, and we—Emily and I—were often responsible for watching over her two younger sisters after school. Well, Emily was responsible for them, and we had been a package deal since second grade. I was sort of along for the ride. We responded to Emily's mom's show of trust by instituting something we called "Wacky Wednesdays," which lasted for about the last two years of our high school careers. The activities of Wacky Wednesdays usually included our other two best friends, Vanessa and Ellen, and ranged from dyeing our hair, taking bubble baths with one another, to inviting lots of people over to drink whatever alcohol we could get our hands on.

We also occasionally took pregnancy tests (always stolen, since they're incredibly expensive, and only Emily really had a job), whether we really needed to or not. What kind of teenager takes a pregnancy test when they don't need to? Everything, even impending, possible but not likely pregnancy, was a potential laugh to us. Pissing on a stick over a toilet was inherently funny. Until it was me doing it for real, because I had a feeling, in my breasts, in my "loins," that something was up. I've only ever had loins when I'm pregnant.

I know that I took the test when there were lots of other people around in the house, but I think I was alone, in Emily's mother's bathroom. I know that afterward I joked about the fact that it was positive to a few people, but I didn't feel like laughing when it actually was. I was buzzed but not drunk.

I felt a deep pit in my stomach, a sickness, a loneliness—

no, an aloneness, that's it. I didn't feel lonely; I felt *alone* in a way that I never had before but still do to this day. The pregnancy test was simply a confirmation of what I'd suspected for a little while, a week or two: my body had felt . . . different and foreign, and I'd allowed my inner voice to whisper, "You're pregnant," in the dead of night once or twice, but I hadn't gone any further than that.

I was taking birth control pills when this happened. I'd been on them consistently for probably a year and a half. I couldn't have said then, and I certainly can't say now, that I had taken every single one of them on time, but even then, at the age of seventeen—I'd been through sex ed; my mother was blunt and open—I knew what all the possible consequences were.

I went outside and sat on the bench in front of Emily's house and started smoking a cigarette. I was still new enough to smoking that every single time I did it, I got an intense head rush. I don't know how many cigarettes I smoked. I remember that Emily came out once. She had a beer in her hand and offered me some. I took it, though I knew I shouldn't. "I guess it doesn't matter, but I feel like I shouldn't drink at all anyway," I told her. I hadn't said, "Hey, I'm thinking about getting an abortion." She assumed that I would, I'm sure. She didn't say, "What are you going to do?" She was probably thinking, "Thank God it's not me," and counting her blessings. That's what I would have been doing, if it were her in my place. I stubbed out the cigarette and went back inside the house. I knew that I had to get it over with, before Emily's mother came home. The pregnancy test, which I kept for at least another two years, was in a Ziploc bag in the back pocket of my jean shorts.

I called my mother, who was staying with my grandmother. She answered the phone because both of my grand-parents were slightly hard of hearing, so she'd probably gotten there first. It was 4:00 or 5:00 in the afternoon. I asked her to go upstairs into one of the bedrooms and to call me back.

"I have to talk to you, call me back."

She called back right away. "You're pregnant, aren't you?"

"Are you kidding?" I answered. I don't know how she knew or why she said it. "Are you psychic?"

Let me say here that I have an excellent memory, particularly for conversations, so much so that people are routinely annoyed with me, my recall of times and places and scenarios, and yes, even exact wording sometimes. And this conversation is even more important than most of the other ones I remember in life. I recall it minutely. I remember breathing into the phone as I listened to her talk.

"Sometimes you just know things," she said, sounding sort of crazy but, of course, she was right, which was the larger point. I guess I didn't really care how she knew. "What do you want to do?" she asked immediately.

What a question. I've thought back on this conversation maybe a thousand times since then. It is the most remarkable framing of a conversation I have ever experienced. In asking this question, my mother conveyed so many things to me: she respected me, wanted to hear what I had to say, and considered me capable of making my own choice. I didn't really process or think about any of this at the time: I was literally hearing "Papa Don't Preach" as a soundtrack in my head and thinking about how limited of a time I had to make a decision. I wasn't sure how much time I had, actually. I didn't know how pregnant I was. I didn't know anyone who had ever had an abortion.

Why did I call her? Plenty of friends in my situation would

not have called their own mothers. In fact, they probably would have called mine. My mother was the cool mom. She was the one we went to and asked what a blow job was. She was the one you asked for advice. She didn't buy me cigarettes, but she turned her head the other way when I smoked hers. It wasn't just that she was young; she was different. And though she often gave good advice, the reasons for her cool-mom status, I know now, were really complicated. I know that much of it was due to her having married so young and being immature in many ways. I know that much of her coolness and willingness to allow regular, parental boundaries be trespassed upon was due to her alcoholism, her lack of fight at important junctures. But it was also, I like to think, somehow part of who she might have been regardless.

It also occurs to me now that this conversation is in some ways very representative of my relationship with my mother overall: we were close and connected, and often, the mother-daughter dynamic was off. Sometimes when I've looked back and thought about my mom, I've judged her harshly (especially as I became a mother myself) for her failure to simply be a parent, to be the one to call the shots consistently and firmly. But this time, this situation, could not really have been handled by a woman who had firmer boundaries. In order to do what she did, and to say what she said, she had to also be a friend to me.

The gist of what I said to her next was something like: I'm too young; I'm scared; I've been drunk a bunch of times; I've been smoking; I'm still in high school. How would I get an abortion? *Can* I get an abortion? Is it a baby yet? (She said yes; I veered toward no.) It was really early, but I didn't know how early. I couldn't remember when my last period was, and they weren't ever that consistent anyway. What if I *do* want to have a baby? What do I do then?

My mother offered to help me raise the baby.

"You could still go to college; I could help; we could all live together," she said. This woman who was so extremely close to finally finishing the decades-long job of raising her own four, without blinking an eye, offered to take on a new one.

All my friends loved my mother, but I suspected they talked about me (and her) behind my back; no one wants a mother who is a "best friend" type exclusively; she might make a good grandmother, but did I really want her to help raise my kid? I couldn't raise a kid; she'd fuck up the kid the way she fucked me up. Wait, was I fucked up? I felt pretty solid most days, actually. I was healthy. I was graduating on time. Then again, I was seventeen, pregnant at my best friend's house on a Wednesday, drinking a beer on the phone and smoking out her dining room window. Fuck this.

This couldn't be my future. I could barely accept its reality in my present.

"I'm going to call Planned Parenthood; I'll get back to you," I said.

Two days later, I had an appointment for an abortion for which my mother would have to give her permission. I remember that the cost of it was about $800, an enormous amount of money for a teenage girl who had only ever held a job for three weeks in her life (at a Little Caesars inside of a Kmart). I didn't even consider if my health insurance would pay for it, because that was under my father's name, and I was terrified that he would somehow see it on a bill. I didn't even get my birth control through my insurance; I paid cash for it every month, watching the pharmacist side-eye me.

Even though my parents were still married, even though my father was still very active in my life, my mother agreed not to tell him when I begged her not to. She agreed to take me to have an abortion and not to tell my father. This made a lot of sense to me in 1995. In 2017, it is sort of incomprehensible to me, but I am still, I have to be honest, thankful for my mother's inability to keep her roles straight. Because she was more of a "friend" to me than she was a wife to my father or a partner in parenting with him, I do not today have a twenty-two-year-old child.

I think in her own terrifically misguided way, my mother was protecting me the only way she knew how. Although we didn't discuss it, she knew the cost of having a family very young. She'd become a mother at the age of twenty, not even out of college yet, to my brother David. Four years later, there was me; sixteen months later, my brother Daniel; and finally, two years after that, my brother John. Boom, boom, boom, boom: a beautiful and not-so-little family.

Though in later years I sometimes felt like she held this—the fact of the abortion, and that she helped me to get it—over me (simply because she often brought it up pointlessly in conversations when she'd been drinking in order to, I felt, hurt me), it was the most selfless act ever performed on my behalf.

It's sort of hard to comprehend how one thing in a person's life can monumentally inform how the rest of their life works out, but in looking back on my own life thus far, there's no doubt that this act, enabled by my mother, is the single most important thing to have happened to me. If I had never had the abortion when I was seventeen, my life would have been indescribably different; who knows if for worse or for better.

But different. I think about this all the time. I thought about it the day that I graduated from high school; on my last day of college; on my first day of graduate school, sitting in orientation. I thought about it the morning my mother died and the afternoon Zelda was born. I think about it sometimes, early in the morning, when I crawl into Zelda's room, the sun barely up, and lay beside her crib as she jostles herself awake, drinking coconut water and touching her belly, making intermittent eye contact with me. She's just a baby: what would my adult child be like? What would *that* life look like? There'd be no Zelda, for one.

Maybe especially because it was Mother's Day, there were protesters outside the abortion clinic in downtown Pittsburgh the sunny morning of my abortion appointment. It was one of those days when there is too much sun, not just for your eyes but for everything, where your whole body feels as though it's squinting and just wants to retreat inside. I'd gotten up very early, having not slept well the night before out of nervousness and fear. I felt that feeling I feel in my stomach when I am tired, a shakiness that is a combination of nerves and a need for food. But I couldn't eat.

The drive from the suburbs to the clinic was maybe forty minutes; my mother was in the front passenger seat, her friend driving. Her friend had been recruited presumably because she too had had an abortion, hers when they'd been roommates together in college. She told us how she'd had to go all the way to New York from Pennsylvania to get hers, because abortion wasn't legal in Pennsylvania at the time. I sat in the back seat solemn and unsure of what I was supposed to feel about any of this.

Being unsure of how you're supposed to feel was the

source of much of my turmoil as a teenager. I felt slight elation at getting the thing over with after a few weeks of nerves and aching sadness; I felt anxiousness at the unknown—I didn't want to run from the fire but rather I wanted to walk into it simply to know what it would feel like, even though it inevitably felt like just that: fire.

What I remember of the rest of that day is tainted by the fact the abortion. The abortion was the most important thing to happen to me, that day, and maybe any other day. Though I have tried to imagine that child into existence many times, the stumbling block of reality—that no child of mine actually existed—stood in the way of really exploring what it could have been like. All I can remember is overwhelmed by what has been, the collective sigh of relief I have felt every day since then, on repeat, skipping like my CD of "Vogue" used to skip in 1990 from too many plays. I can never quite get over how *good* I felt after that procedure.

I make excuses for myself now, because I was basically a kid, but I have to say that I still do feel that sense of relief at not being pregnant any longer. My body was once again all my own, the invasion was over, and I felt, to the extent that a seventeen-year-old can, a new lease on life. Anything, it seemed, was suddenly possible, all because I had undergone, without anesthesia ("Fuck that, I'll stay awake, I'm fine"), a short—it couldn't have lasted longer than ten minutes— abortion, ending my pregnancy at seven weeks. It wasn't just a possible baby that I aborted that day but a whole series of possibilities that died and were reborn there in those few minutes while I lay on my back, looking up at a slowly rotating mobile that had silver stars and sheep on it. The lighting was pulled way down low, and there might have been soft music piped in. Though the clinic was a bustling, busy place (clearly the weekends were booming), the room where the procedure itself was performed was quiet and calm and empty: nothing betrayed what went down in there, until I craned my neck around and spied the equipment that did the job.

Only much later in life, when the internet had become part of my daily life, did I investigate what this procedure actually entailed. I remember it as mildly uncomfortable, mentally challenging, and emotionally . . . well. The thing about this, for me, was that the relief washed away almost any other emotion. As I sat in the little recovery room, back in my own clothes in a huge recliner, sipping orange juice from a straw stuffed into a little cardboard carton, I felt almost as though I could cry. But no one else—none of the other girls, all of them young like me, with the exception of one woman who seemed impossibly old who I wondered about just then, and who seemed to me the saddest of us all—seemed upset. "I'll be sad later," I thought, just wanting to get through the door and back to my mother.

But I'm still waiting for that wash of feeling. I feel a lot of emotion now for my mother and for what it must have taken for her, a forty-two-year-old Catholic woman who had been married since she was twenty, to take her only daughter into the city and get her an abortion. I feel proud of her for having done it for me, for what are obviously selfish reasons. I feel confusion that she did do it, not knowing if I could do the same. I feel some anger for her allowing me to keep it from my father, thus engendering what was a serious but ultimately positive thing for me with a shroud of dark secrecy that I see now it didn't have to have had. I could have told him, and she was the only person who could have made me feel it was okay to do so. Instead, she chose the easier path, the one that I desired so much in the moment and worried over so much later on. What I don't feel, in any part of me, is regret about the abortion.

And I like to think, though I can't and won't ever know, that my mother knew then what is so obvious to me now: that the best decision I ever made was made possible only by that one act of quiet, secret selflessness on her part. She wouldn't win any Mother of the Year awards for doing it; she wouldn't be admired by her other friends who were mothers or by her family—that's why she didn't tell anyone she was doing it— but she did it just the same, I assume because she knew what it would be worth to me, then and always.

My mother, who was only a few years older than I am now when she made that choice, never met her granddaughter or her son-in-law. She never knew me as a married woman or as a mother, and really, she barely knew me as an adult. And though much in my life has changed in the decade since she died, nothing has changed as much as my relationship with her. And in some ways, her dying led me here: the space she left behind opened a new place for me to make new things; happier things and, in many ways, better ones.

And by the time I did become a mother, at the age of thirty-six, on a Tuesday in February, more than three years ago, I thought that my relationship with my mother had been what it was going to be for the rest of time. After all, isn't that what being dead means?

CHAPTER 2

• • •

My mother, she would be the first to brag proudly, was great at having children. She excelled at easy pregnancies: no sickness, no drugs necessary. She didn't gain much weight; we were just little basketballs on her tiny frame, and my brothers and I were all normal-size, perfectly healthy babies at birth. My aunt told me not long ago that she remembered the family talking about how my dad had to rush to the hospital right when she went into labor because otherwise he'd miss our births. She recovered easily; she never had a C-section or a pregnancy-related illness.

"Having babies is easy!" my mother said to me when I was fourteen or fifteen, when I expressed horror after viewing the PBS film *The Miracle of Life* in health class. She reveled in my disgust at the prospect. "Babies are easy, really," she said. "Kids are harder. But babies? Psssssh."

Maybe the fact that my mother was so excellent at the process of getting pregnant, staying pregnant, giving birth, and caring for newborns was what catapulted her into her life as a mother of four by the age of twenty-nine. Maybe it was just Catholics being bad at birth control. But as I moved shakily, hesitantly, and suspiciously into my own bout of motherhood, that fact, that my mother had thought it was barely a blip and certainly nothing worth complaining about, was often in the back of my mind.

Because my pregnancy, let me be clear, kind of sucked. And in another place and time before modern medicine, I'd probably have ended up dead. Almost definitely. Or Zelda wouldn't have made it. But here we are now; I'm alive and well enough to complain about it. A lot.

My ambivalence about having a child was fading, but my body still seemed unsure. My own pregnancy, unlike my mother's, never settled into an easy groove that let me grow comfortable. Instead, I progressed through it in a haze of complications, my body feeling as though it were constantly under attack.

The day I found out I was pregnant, I calculated it to be about six weeks. My doctor didn't want to see me until nine weeks, which is when a heartbeat is usually detectable and can rule out early miscarriages, so I made an appointment and plotted out how to wait out that time, taking pains to avoid telling anyone, not even really daring to think about the time beyond the next few weeks. Josh was excited, but he followed my lead. Wait and see.

A week and a half after I made the appointment, so far then in the future, I felt a familiar feeling—a sudden wetness— that, because I was now pregnant, seemed bad. I went into the bathroom and saw what I knew and feared I would see: blood.

"I think it's just . . . gone," I said to Josh when I came out of the bathroom. I was crying, but only a little bit, because I didn't know if it was gone. Was I still pregnant? I'd been pregnant knowingly for only two weeks. . . . Was I supposed to be sad?

I thought of the possible baby in my future for a second.

"Call the doctor," Josh said. Oh. Right. The doctor. Josh was so much smarter than me.

I went in that day, alone, because Josh had a meeting that he couldn't cancel, and I assured him I was just fine to go on my own. My first visit with my obstetrician, a guy I didn't know but who had been recommended via email by my GP, was because I was bleeding. Not the happy circumstance I'd been expecting and weeks earlier than I thought, but there I was, sitting in a room, waiting for him to come in, staring at a chart that listed the statistical likelihood of having a baby with Down syndrome based on maternal age. I noted that the likelihood really skyrocketed right around thirty-five before he came in.

"There we go," Dr. Moritz said as he performed my ultrasound, declaring, "A heartbeat." The fetus was, for now, alive. It didn't sound like a heartbeat. It was muddled and watered down. It was so fast.

"That's good, right?"

"That's very good!" He smiled at me. I wondered if he thought maybe I was not very bright before I remembered he saw women like me in these circumstances every day. This was no big deal for him; he could be relaxed and matter-of-fact about the whole thing. My whole thing. My fetus. I realized while sitting there, for the first time, how desperately I wanted it to survive. Hours earlier I'd told myself it would be fine if I lost it, but suddenly, that wasn't true at all. I didn't yet think of it as a baby, but it was more than nothing. A desire, a biological need for it to survive and be protected by me, had appeared from . . . nowhere.

"Moving forward from today," he said, "you have a fifty-fifty chance of losing the pregnancy." This sounded bad, of course. Anytime a woman—maybe my age was a factor, but maybe not, I don't know—bleeds early in her pregnancy for unknown reasons, the odds are about fifty-fifty that she'll miscarry. The longer you go without bleeding, the odds of keeping it increase. Fifty-fifty. Not bad. But not good. He explained all of this in thirty seconds.

"It's okay," he said, patting my shoulder. But he didn't seem overly concerned, either.

"Does this happen a lot?" I asked, comforted at the imagined prospect that I might be one of many.

"Yes, women get pregnant all the time," he said, straight-faced, before breaking into a smile. "It's okay"—he patted my shoulder again—"the best thing you can do is not worry."

To this, I mentally said, "LOL." Worrying is what I do. My anxious energy pushes me through every day, every piece of work, every holiday meal for twenty-four people. Aggressive worrying is how I operate.

"I'll try," I said with a smile, looking out the window at the buildings across the street. I wanted to be out on the street again, not there in that office, wondering when I would bleed again.

I got lucky in the doctor department. Dr. Moritz was the right choice. Over the course of the pregnancy we would see him, almost always Josh and me together, many more times than a woman with a normal pregnancy sees her obstetrician. He was, like Josh, a joker in the face of struggle and fear. But Josh couldn't joke about this, so Dr. Moritz was there to do some of the work for us.

"Take your vitamins," he said, clearly wrapping up our visit.

"Every time you bleed, you reset the clock," he said, and though I never wanted things to be candy coated, even I could admit that these odds seemed . . . bad. "Don't worry, take multivitamins, and don't worry," he said. "This part isn't up to you, and you're not in control."

It was the absolute best advice I have ever received about pregnancy and, in some ways, motherhood, too.

◆　◆　◆

I bled three more times over the course of my first trimester, and yet, every time, I went in to see the doctor, squeezed in between other, scheduled appointments, and there was that sound, the heartbeat. I couldn't hear the heartbeat at home when I woke up at 6:00 a.m. to the now-familiar feeling that I had gotten my period, even though I was pregnant. I wasn't sure. I had to go see: Is it alive?

"Nothing is in my control" became my mantra.

My husband was supportive, but as a woman whose body tenuously held on to pregnancy against what seemed to be increasingly pushy and inhospitable conditions, I can tell you that I felt quite alone in that period. Dr. Moritz advised us to wait longer than normal to tell people. Usually, they'll tell you to wait until twelve weeks. He said wait until sixteen or so if we could. Already, it seemed, we might be at some disadvantage: the pregnancy, always high risk because of "advanced maternal age" (I was, after all, thirty-six years old!) now seemed to be truly under fire. This didn't seem as though it would last. It really didn't. And I don't count on things that aren't going to last. I couldn't be optimistic, not then. Optimism was blindness.

It seemed more likely to me that I would end this phase without a baby than with. Simply put, much of my pregnancy really didn't feel like pregnancy. It felt like an extended possibility of miscarriage, where some days I even just wished for it to get over with already, so sure did it seem that I wouldn't hold on to it.

But I did. Or, more accurately, it held on to me. She held on.

In fact, though I felt kind of funereal in my heart, every early appointment progressed just fine. The fetus was growing, developing at a completely normal rate. The blood was inexplicable, the fetus—the baby, if you're an antiabortionist—seemed totally fine, happy as a pea, a bean, a brussels sprout, just hanging on in there, no awareness that all day every day for me, her mother-to-be, was "Oh shit, oh shit, oh shit!" And yet, every few weeks, there was a little trickle of blood, for seemingly no reason, which I took as an attack against me and my recently acquired hopes and dreams of motherhood.

I made no plans; I brainstormed no names. I staked out my territory, waiting. The summer passed us quickly, and gradually, we allowed ourselves to tell close friends and family.

I told my father much too early. I even told him about the blood. "I'm not sure; it might not stay," I said. I didn't know what he knew of gynecology. We told Josh's parents. We told his brother, who was getting married just then, in the midst of all this. I carried it like a secret, but one that I couldn't even admit to myself.

We can tell "the kind of people we won't mind telling if it goes away," I wrote to myself in my journal, a new one I had started expressly to document the pregnancy. The individual pages were large—eleven by seventeen—but there weren't very many of them. I didn't choose it consciously, but looking back at it now, it's clear to me that I didn't think this was gonna last. I felt sure, really, that it wouldn't.

I'd been ambivalent for so much of my life about having a child, and even once I'd decided that I wanted one, I'd cried tears of anguish or fear at the prospect of a baby. But now that I was pregnant, I wanted to hang on, to have the baby. I wanted the pregnancy to stay.

And it did. The months wore on. We did scans and drew blood and went through genetic screening to see if we carried anything that might be passed on. My mother-in-law was with me when I did the genetic counseling. When they asked if I'd miscarried or aborted, I said, "One miscarriage." Not true: I had to run back in and tell them I had lied.

The many tests didn't find anything abnormal, which, that early in the pregnancy, when they do find things, are often very serious. We aced the tests, all the while feeling under threat. I kept bleeding.

A few days after the genetic screening, the counselor called me from the hospital in the middle of the afternoon. I was standing in the huge open office I worked in, surrounded by twenty or thirty other people. We were in the middle of a week of all-hands meetings, and writers had traveled from all over the parts of the world where they normally worked to be there. Josh and I worked together, and he was in his office across the room. I could see him through the glass. I texted him from across the office: "They wanna know if we want to know if it's a boy or a girl." "Go for it," he responded as I stood waiting there at my desk, ready to call them back.

"You're having a girl," the counselor said.

Josh told everyone in the office moments later that I was going to have a baby. A rare thing, in a roomful of bloggers, mostly men, mostly under the age of thirty.

Learning this, that we were going to have a girl, somehow made my pregnancy real in a way that it hadn't felt before: Here was information I could snag on to and hold. Here was something I could imagine around. My baby was going to be a girl. I was a few weeks into my second trimester, and everything was going fine.

*   *   *

Then followed a few fairly blissful weeks. I never really had morning sickness, I felt just fine, and I wasn't yet so large that I felt encumbered simply by existing and taking up too much space. We moved into the fall—our daughter was expected at the end of February—happily. I finally allowed myself for the first time to really enjoy the concept of having a baby. I started researching cribs and strollers, making plans to clean out the spare bedroom, which would now be the nursery. I worked, and I planned. I allowed myself the luxury—one I had always avoided—of thinking, and even looking forward to, the future. I allowed myself to hope and to plan, things that have often been very hard for me even in the presence of great reason to hope. I wanted my hopefulness to last, and I wanted to share it.

I have always approached life with a certain sense of wariness, not because I'm naturally cynical but because often, expecting the worst can mean that your expectations cannot be over-wrought. I remember a long-ago childhood conversation with Emily in which she told me, "Things never live up to how I imagine them, in my mind, the way I see something; it's always better than what actually happens." I got that feeling completely, but I didn't necessarily share it. I often approached things from the opposite side: I didn't play things up or out in my mind. I expected nothing. And so occasionally I was pleasantly surprised when cool things happened, or when a party turned out to be fun instead of boring or awkward. I didn't try to make friends, but sometimes I found a special person I connected with.

But with the progress of my pregnancy, I not only allowed myself to feel excitement at the prospect of the future, I embraced it. I wanted to meet this kid, badly, because for the first time, my imagination wasn't filling in anything for me: I couldn't even grasp at a basic outline, and each time she grew on the sonograms I got every two or three weeks, they didn't really help me fill in the space. "I have no idea what she'll be like," I said to the air as I stood in the kitchen, stirring a pot of something for dinner. I couldn't imagine her yet, and not knowing was so hard but so full of possibility. I imagined her then as a person, a wonderful, beautiful, vague, and poorly drawn person, but a person nonetheless.

I became a different, less taciturn being temporarily. "I'm pregnant" I started saying to random New Yorkers on the street or on the subway. "I can see that," one of them once deadpanned back to me. I didn't care; I was already floating up the stairs toward the street, and my feet didn't even touch the pavement. I was feeling fine. Just fine.

I started buying her books. Maybe it made sense to buy

her clothes or practical things first, but I started with what I loved and what I had ideas about. I bought her a *Little House on the Prairie* set, among other "great books" of my youth: *Island of the Blue Dolphins, The Monster at the End of This Book, Madeline, The Snowy Day, The Phantom Tollbooth.* Because I didn't envision her as a specific person, she seemed ageless, and so I purchased whatever I wanted. I didn't need baby books; she could read more advanced material. I was, without thinking about it, already trying to shape the person I imagined her to be or the one I'd like her to be. I imagined her as a book lover, like myself. These were impractical first purchases. Long before I thought of bottles or onesies or diapers, I thought of books.

I didn't worry too much about what the experience of birth would be like, and I didn't worry about what it would be like to have a baby. For the first time in my life, I felt as though I was really living almost entirely in the present. I knew that it couldn't go on forever. But I tried to enjoy it while I could.

In hindsight, it's hard to complain or even to linger over any one complication, because my daughter was born and she was healthy and beautiful. But in truth, my pregnancy was pretty miserable. As I moved into the second trimester, I began to feel very tired, and I gained weight very quickly. I remember being offended the first time the doctor said something to me about watching what I ate. I'd read about these kinds of warnings. I wasn't overeating; I was doing everything just like I was supposed to! I'm a vegetarian, and I generally eat well anyway, and now I was drinking lots of water and paying attention to everything I ingested. What did he mean I should "be careful"?

But he was right: I had gained weight alarmingly fast.

Reading my chart now, it's clear that there was a problem: I started at 135 and then edged over to 140 in the first three months. But less than two weeks later, I was nearly at 150. By the time I gave birth, I weighed 199 pounds. But it wasn't from food.

Around the twentieth week of my pregnancy, at one of our routine checkups, I asked about birthing classes. I was worried that Josh, whose tolerance for unenjoyable activities he views as a waste of time can be very low, would not fare well in a class with other participants, and I was hoping we could have something private, maybe at home, even if it costed more.

"Hire a doula," Dr. Moritz said, "and then you don't even have to bother with the birth classes at all." At various points throughout the pregnancy, this obstetrician truly seemed like a magician, and this was one of those times. I felt relief wash over me as the anxiety about what that fucking class would be like melted away. We could put it off! We could read a book or watch a YouTube video about birth. Our doctor was in a documentary about birth—*The Business of Being Born*—and we could just view that one night, for fun. But we never watched it. "I could figure it out," I thought. "How hard could it be?"

That's what I told myself as I put off reading books about the process of birth, opting instead for those about child-rearing and baby caring. I mired myself in the details of sleep training and feeding, of identifying ailments and fevers and rashes. I studied the CDC's immunization schedules and did research on pediatricians.

What I didn't do was make a birth plan.

A birth plan is one of those things that no one has heard

of until they're pregnant, and then suddenly everyone has them when they are. "How do you want to give birth?" Dr. Moritz asked me very early on. A fair enough question, one that I'm sure most women have an answer for.

"I-in a hospital," I stammered.

"Okay, good. Good to know." He laughed. "Not everyone does!"

"I mean, I can just imagine what a mess it would be. Even thinking about it is upsetting," I said, getting lost in the moment of considering a home birth. "The dog barking, the FedEx guy ringing the doorbell." It was sudden—I'd never considered such a thing, and then in seconds I was dead set against it.

A birth plan, I learned, was my sketch of an ideal way for things to go down. Dr. Moritz didn't seem too big on the concept, as he was the one, after all, who said, "Nothing is in your control," but he encouraged me to go for it if I wanted. "Plan away," he said. I remained suspicious and pragmatic and maybe just a little superstitious. So I strenuously avoided developing a birth plan.

When the doula popped over to our place, I remember so distinctly having that first conversation.

"Do you want to avoid pain medication during labor? Do you want a natural birth?" she asked.

"I guess . . . so?" I said, standing in our kitchen, looking up at the ceiling. "I have a pretty high tolerance for pain, and the competitive person inside me sort of likes the sound of that," I went on nervously. I hadn't really thought about it. That was clear.

"Why would you want that?" Josh almost yelled. "That's incredibly dumb! Who wants more pain?" he exclaimed.

"You should do what you want, though." He turned the corner as quickly as always.

"Here's the thing," the doula said, looking me deep in the eyes. "If you go into the labor unsure of what you want, you will almost certainly end up with medication or interventions of some kind."

Interventions sounded bad. But after she left, Josh and I had a long conversation.

"You don't have to be a hero for me," he said.

"I can so very much do this without any medication," I said. I had caught a glimpse of that beautiful area where privileged mothers can push out a baby without any pain medication in the full care of a great, modern, New York City hospital, feeling empowered and emboldened, and I wanted it. I thought of my mother, imagined her slipping out four kids, telling me, "It's nothing." I felt, now that I knew there was supposedly some better way to give birth (without drugs) in the minds of doulas and midwives and Brooklyn mom groups, challenged by the idea, even if I couldn't explain why it would be "better" at all.

"Why would you choose pain over less pain?" Josh asked.

None of this, he said, had to do with the baby. All of it was about me. He was right. She had her own plans.

The baby, whom we would later name Zelda, was breech. We knew that from pretty early on; she'd seemed comfortable just hanging out in the "wrong position." Breech, I was aware, meant that if she didn't turn, we'd probably not have a "natural" birth. Breech meant C-section. Breech meant drugs. But there was "nothing to worry about," everyone assured me. Babies turn all the time! It was a breezy "Oh, she's breech" at first, the doctor assuring me there was "plenty of time" for her to turn. But by thirty-five weeks, she wasn't just breech; she was transverse.

Transverse in Latin means, I think, "sideways." The sonogram images of her in this stage are very cute: she's laying, yes, sideways, as if my lower body were her couch, her feet pushed against the left side of my abdomen, her head pushing against the right. As she grew larger, comfortably snug against me, we could see the outline of her head pushing out the side of my body, like an alien trying to emerge. It hurt. A lot. By the end, I thought I could feel every time she turned her head. Doing things—anything—became agony. Though I worked until days before I gave birth, I worked from home in the final months, because it became ever-increasingly clear that I was getting sick. And I was still getting fatter.

As I said, I started pregnancy at 135 pounds. I see the chart now, and it fills me with anxiety, not because the numbers the nurse copied from the scale during each visit got so large, but because in hindsight it was clear that something wasn't right.

In fact, rapid weight gain is only one sign of preeclampsia, but it wasn't one that I was predisposed to be suspicious of: I was supposed to gain weight, right?

The first sign was when I noticed something was wrong with my feet. I was getting out of bed one morning and swung my feet over the side of the bed. I looked down at them, and they looked fat. They looked like sausages, just slightly more toes and less angles than I expected. I shoved my feet into my shoes: they fit, but barely. I have been a size 8 since I was fifteen. By the end of my pregnancy I was a 9.5 wide if I was lucky: I couldn't really get shoes on anymore. I emailed my doctor, and he said he would take a look the next time I was in. That was in early September, nearly six months before my daughter was due. It was mild, and when I saw him he didn't seem particularly worried. He warned me to stay hydrated and to try to stay off my feet.

"I'm only four months pregnant!" I laughed.

The swelling came and went at first, but again, in hindsight, it was some kind of progression: each time it came back, it was a little worse. I began to tire a lot easier, and my weight gains seemed to ramp up. But by mid-October, I was monitoring my blood pressure at home a few times a day and emailing it to my doctor. Because it was high.

And one morning in November, sitting in Dr. Moritz's office alone because my husband was at work, I stared across the room to the mirror on the wall at myself while waiting for him. When he walked in, I said, "Does my face look swollen to you?"

It did.

He sent me home with a large jug that I was to pee in for twenty-four hours and then take back to the hospital with me to test for protein in my urine, one of the signs of preeclampsia. I can't remember when he actually brought up that word, but preeclampsia is a condition often seen in pregnant women that is mainly characterized by high blood pressure and protein in your urine and, often, sudden weight gain. It used to be, sometimes, fatal. I knew this because I had watched *Downton Abbey*. Sybil died an agonizing death from her preeclampsia. If it's not caught, seizures can follow. My blood pressure was high, I was gaining weight and retaining water, my daughter was transverse. But I passed. It was negative. My doctor had monitored all of this closely, never really alarming me, but keeping us aware that this was not exactly an ideal situation. I kept monitoring my blood pressure at home a few times a day. It fluctuated from a little above normal to quite high. I felt like shit; I was worried all the time. And the fetus? She was doing just fine.

Early one morning, a month and ten days before my daughter was due, I felt what I could only describe as contractions. I emailed the doctor. "Don't worry," he wrote back almost immediately, "but go to Labor and Delivery."

Ha! Don't worry, but head to the hospital. The nurse in L&D seemed sure I wasn't having anything more than little early-warning contractions—until she strapped the monitors on me. My baby was fine, her heartbeat was strong, but I was indeed having fairly strong contractions. They pumped me full of fluids, hoping that I was simply dehydrated, which I learned could cause contractions. Eventually, after sitting in a hospital bed for six hours, the contractions subsided, though not completely. I was thirty-five weeks pregnant, and they told me it was possible, though not likely, that I would feel the contractions on and off until my daughter was born.

And I did. It was sometimes a simple, dull background noise, but others were a severe, almost toothache pain, worse than menstrual cramps and mentally anguishing. I worried I was going into labor constantly. I couldn't tell anymore what was normal, and my daughter remained stubbornly in a bad position. I tried to keep my complaints to myself. Many of my friends were childless, and anytime I described the feelings aloud, they became alarmed. But I'd been told so many times not to worry, which was impossible, so I settled for trying not to worry anyone else. I complained to Josh only when necessary, though I also worried about worrying him.

This state of affairs didn't dampen my excitement completely, but it did bring me back into more well-worn territory, where I felt anxious and unsure that everything would turn out all right.

Finally, a week or so later, I went in for a checkup, probably around thirty-six weeks, I weighed in at 191 pounds, and my blood pressure was above normal but not terrible. I was having contractions.

"If you didn't know this already," Dr. Moritz said, "it's unlikely that she is going to turn into the correct position. Now," he went on, "the entire game is seeing how close we can get you to forty weeks." But I think he knew that she would likely need to come out before then, around thirty-seven weeks, which is when a baby is finally considered "full term."

By then, preeclampsia was unquestionable. The best way to get rid of preeclampsia is to have the baby. My daughter was transverse. She was not going to be born "naturally," a description of birth that I rejected by then. Natural as opposed to . . . what? Imaginary concepts of natural birth vs. C-sections and drugs slipped out of the conversation as I was faced with reality: I wasn't being offered a choice because there wasn't one. The baby was in a position that meant she couldn't be labored out on her own without one of us dying or causing an emergency medical situation, and my preeclampsia made it extremely unlikely that I could wait until labor arrived anyway. I think of this now and feel a little terrified in hindsight, but at the time, I felt relieved to hear that we were nearing the end. I felt as though we would do better, the baby and I, if she was outside my body, which seemed to be turning on us both.

The first day of officially hitting thirty-seven weeks was a Monday, the first one in February. I woke up at dawn to terrible cramps. I had an appointment at 2:30 that afternoon. The last email I sent to the doctor was at 1:51 p.m. "My contractions are worse in the morning, I think," I wrote. "I'll see you soon."

An hour later, he told me to go home, lay down, and come back to the hospital early the next morning to have my daughter born, via C-section.

◆　◆　◆

So we did just that. She was born at 1:45 p.m. after a mostly painless epidural and a painless C-section. I never went into labor, and I never pushed even once, but I can't say that I have ever felt, for one second, like I missed out on anything. I'm not saying that in some completely imaginary, otherworld best-case scenario I wouldn't have done it differently; I might have. But this is the only birth I have known or seen, and I remember it in excruciating detail. What more could a mother ask for? An unnatural, beautiful birth.

I don't know the details of my own birth. I know that my mother thought I was a girl but wasn't sure and that I was a week late. I don't know what her labor was like, though if her accounts of "birth" in general are any indication, my guess is it was easy and complication-free. I don't know, to be honest, if she breast-fed me. It simply never came up while she was alive, and though I've wished her back to life many times since my daughter was born, it was never to learn how I came into the world. I am here, and that's enough.

And that was how I felt about Zelda when she arrived: I could recount the details, I remember them minutely, but they weren't important at the time. She was here.

I weighed 199 pounds the day that I checked into the

hospital in February of 2014 to have Zelda. I was feeling very bad: much of my weight (though less than I would have liked, to be honest) was water, and that is painful to carry. I felt as though the skin on my swollen feet and ankles and hands was going to split open. My face was swollen, my neck was fat. All of me felt unwell and overwhelmed. My daughter was literally sideways and backward. I could see her head sticking out the right side of my stomach at all times. I'd like to say that I was overwhelmed with worry about her, and I was, to some extent.

But I didn't know her yet. I knew me. And I wanted her out.

I checked in and faced an apparently normal wall of paperwork. I signed forms giving them the right to do whatever needed to be done in emergency situations. "Isn't this an emergency?" I wondered. It wasn't. There were other, far worse ways that this could all go down. I distinctly remember the form that asked if I wanted to be put to sleep for the procedure, because this wasn't an option I realized was even offered any longer.

"I could literally peace out on this? LOL," I thought, as I declined. I'm not a fan of anesthesia or even of painkillers, to be honest. I assumed the epidural would be enough to get me through the day. My mother had been awake for all of our births. Surely I could handle this.

At some point they split up my husband and me; at some point I was put on a hospital bed that they started wheeling me around to various rooms on. I had to be wheeled around, they told me. I couldn't walk into the operating room. I wanted to. I was still me. "Can I walk in?" I asked. "You can't," the kind attendant said as he wheeled me in, an invalid perfectly capable of walking.

I've learned since that day that experiences with epidurals vary pretty wildly. Mine was uneventful and not painful. I remember the exact sensation of it kicking in. "I feel static-y, like there's static inside my whole body," I said happily to the people in the OR. I faded out, drifting almost to sleep. "Little too much there, ha-ha," one of them said as they pulled me back from wherever I'd been off to. I wanted to go away, then, briefly. I hadn't had a drink in so long; I'd been so conscious and aware of every little thing. Just for a second, as I felt the drugs overwhelm me, I thought, "Let me go." They brought me back.

"Do you have a name for the baby?" another guy, somewhere up around my head, asked me. I was staring at the ceiling, which was probably twelve or thirteen or twenty-five feet high. The room was cold and bright and vast. "Yes," I said, not sure if I should tell him or not. "Zelda," I blurted out, realizing for the first time that that would be her name. We'd basically decided it already, but I don't think we'd told anyone before, and there I was, telling this guy I couldn't even see, this man I didn't know. I felt so close to him. Where the fuck was he? I tried to turn my head.

"I can't feel my legs," I said.

"You're not supposed to," someone said.

"You know how one person can make or break an entire name?" I asked aloud.

"What do you mean?"

"I mean like how Hitler just ruined Adolf. You can't name a kid Adolf now."

Silence.

At some point Dr. Moritz came in, and I saw him in a different light than I had in the preceding months. I liked him; he was funny and nice and warm. My husband, who came in with him, liked him, too. They were cracking jokes, and suddenly I realized there was a huge divide between me and them: "I'm the only person in this room today on the verge of dying," I thought. "The chances are very low, like, sliver chances," I told myself, "but they're so much higher than theirs that we're not on the same timeline. I'm alone in a really particular way right now." I thought this. I was alone.

Except I wasn't: she, my daughter, not yet Zelda but no longer quite Laura, was on my timeline, in my zone, too. She could die as well, I knew, though I didn't want to think of that. We could blaze out together; in fact, the whole reason we were there in that operating room, at thirty-seven weeks deep into the pregnancy, so much earlier than expected, was that one or both of us was going to be in some serious shit if we didn't all take action. We, she and I, spending our last moments in the same body together, my body, we were on the same timeline, alone in that room. I was taking back my body and giving her her own timeline.

In previous centuries, one of us, probably both of us, would have been goners. I knew this. There are so many goners in my family tree. They're hard to find, because dead babies at birth in history rarely even get names. They don't get gravestones; it's expensive, and nature is what it is. In nature, I would be dead. Instead, I have this beautiful doctor, these people helping me. I would have died. She would have died. I know this.

And I was aware of that when I looked at my husband, and more so at my doctor: here was the man who would open me up and pull my daughter out.

Moments later, Josh made some joke—I can't remember about what but am too stubborn to go and ask him for fear that he will realize my memory isn't infallible—and that joke was greeted tersely by Dr. Moritz: "This is my stage," he said to Josh. I had a great view of him, as he was directly above me, while Josh sat on a stool behind my right shoulder. "I make the jokes here."

For some reason, his making that clear reassured me. I was scared, but I couldn't tense up my body because I couldn't feel anything. I don't know where my hands were. What were my hands doing? They hadn't tied them down. Or maybe they did? They didn't. But what were they doing? Did they tie my hands down?

Either right before or right after Zelda was "born," Josh leaned over and whispered into my ear, "I'm afraid you're going to die, there's so much blood." On the one hand, this seems, in hindsight, a really insane thing for him to have said to me, the person who was laying there, just trying to stay alive. On the other, it let the air out of the whole thing: "Me too," I said. "But I'm okay; I feel fine." I had someone to re-assure. That felt good. It felt like living.

Zelda was born, as I said, at 1:45 p.m., only ten minutes or so after they'd rolled me into that room. Her umbilical cord was wrapped around her neck—"Three times!" Dr. Moritz marveled—but she was breathing, a little silent, a sort of bluish alien thing. They held her over the sheet that divided me from my internal organs on display, and I looked at her for the first time, still thinking about myself primarily. That mode of being—where I was mentally first—was going to end hard and fast in less than twenty-four hours, but I didn't know any other way yet. I didn't quite think on her behalf, and so she still seemed like a foreign object to me. Not really so far off the mark, honestly: a just-born baby is barely human, only partly among us. She was whisked over to the other side of the room to be tested and wiped off, to have her cord cut and to be dressed. Josh went with her for a moment but wandered back to stay with me while I was sewn up or whatever it was they were doing to me. I didn't know who cut the cord.

I heard the baby cry and tried to look around to see her, craning my neck wildly.

"She's okay," Josh said. And she was: she was okay. Her Apgar scores were shit, but she was doing just fine. Her lungs worked, and she was, at six pounds, nine ounces, not even small for a baby who was three weeks early.

"Do we want to call her Zelda? Are we sure?" Josh asked.

"I'm sure," I said back.

And so there we were. Three of us.

I was moved to a middle waiting room, where other women who have also just given birth were being stored, too. We would have a private hospital room for the three of us later. I didn't know where anybody was, but my phone and a few other personal effects had appeared from somewhere. I texted my father. I lay back on the bed. I felt fine.

Josh reappeared, came to check on me.

"She's so beautiful," he said. "We gave her a bath," he told me.

"Where is she?" I asked. He left.

Eventually, probably less than an hour later, they wheeled me down the hall and into our room. Zelda was there, and they unswaddled her to lay her on my chest. She was so tiny and beet red. She was hot to the touch. She was awake and looking at me. She could see me. I could see her. She held my finger, which seemed just impossible. How could a baby hold a finger?

These are mundane and universal observations, tearjerker moments about the birth of a baby. Their universality is what I valued: after a tough pregnancy, we were at a new beginning. The scoreboard was reset. We were just like everyone else.

People have asked me on a few occasions if I had any regrets about the way Zelda was born. The C-section, they mean. Those people, parents mostly, have a lot of opinions, and one of those opinions is that birth, especially in the United States, has become too "medicalized." In the years since Zelda's birth, I've thought about this more than I probably should have.

What they call "natural" birth, the kind of birth that often eschews pain medication, should never include a C-section. The C-section, to a natural birth advocate, is the worst-case scenario.

My opinion, the only opinion I find to be acceptable, has always been that the worst-case scenario is a dead mother or baby or both. I have never felt disappointed about my "birth experience," mostly because I didn't really consider it an "experience."

I never formed many strong opinions about what would be ideal, I simply took what came toward me and tried to accept and make the best of it. People fool themselves into believing that the birth of their child is about them. It's not: it's about their children. They're the ones being pushed or pulled out. We owe them a safe arrival. And so, that's what we gave her. I didn't want surgery, but we don't often get what we want, and I am not a doctor. I do not presume to have a better solution to a breech baby and a preeclamptic mother.

My birth experience, such as it was, was about the best thing I could have imagined.

And even though I felt lonely without my mother, that day in February will always be what I consider to be the best day of my life. A turning point. A new beginning. And the day that I met my daughter for the first time.

When people ask if I was disappointed by my birth experience, I want to tell them to fuck off. I want to scream at them and tell them they're terrible people who don't know anything, that they're one step away from vaccine deniers.

Instead I just say, "No. Were you?"

◆　◆　◆

We left the hospital at 5:30 p.m. the next day in advance of a snowstorm. February is arguably the worst month of the year in New York City. It is often bitterly cold, snowy, and generally grungy. Happily, however, it is also the month of the year that the fewest babies are born. I assume this is because February is the shortest month, but either way, the hospital, the busiest for births in New York City, was actually pretty quiet. We got our own private room at the end of a quiet hallway, and we hunkered down for what we assumed would be a few days but turned out to be only about twenty-four hours.

The rest of the stay passed in a weird blur that was almost all positive. The hospital food was good, and we had a private room, so the three of us slept together. "Slept" is a funny term for whatever it was we were doing in that time, awake every fifteen minutes, but we held together. The baby was beautiful. She was healthy. She was eating.

I recuperated easily. So easily, in fact, that the doctor warned me that I must take my medicine every six hours, like clockwork, because I'd refused the prescribed Percocet and insisted on taking only a large dose of ibuprofen. "If you don't take it every six hours, you'll pay," the nurses kept telling me. My fear of becoming an opioid addict overcame my worry about postpartum pain. We filled the Percocet prescription "just in case," but I never took a single one. Maybe I was like my mother after all: at least the postpartum period seemed not so bad for me, and I'd heard horror stories from women about pain and barely being able to walk. This seemed suddenly doable to me.

I was up and walking around by 11:00 the morning after Zelda was born, motivated by some hormones I couldn't name and didn't care about; I was ready to get on with it. The nurses didn't exactly marvel, but they certainly commented on it when they saw me walk out the door of our room, dressed in sweat pants. "I'm just going for a stroll," I said, looking in at the nursery to my left where several newborn babies lay. I walked all the way to the end of the hall, to the window. It was going to snow. I felt bad physically—just drained. The epidural had not totally worn off. I could walk and move, but I was numb in my middle. I've never liked being away from home, not even if the alternative is a luxury hotel or a new, exotic locale; within a matter of hours I am dreaming of the emotional comfort of home. I've traveled enough to learn to ignore those little calls, of my apartment or my own bed, my books and my kitchen, but I felt this acutely in the hospital after Zelda's birth, just a few miles from home.

Dr. Moritz came in early that afternoon to look at my incision and declared it beautiful and healing.

"You will barely know it happened," he said, as he confirmed that I could go home if I wanted to.

"What about the baby?" I asked.

"Not my territory," he said, waving off my suggestion that he take a look at her. "The pediatricians will tell you." He was joking but not: he dealt with me, and someone else handled my daughter. We were two things now; I'd just forgotten that again. "Oh, right," I thought. "She has her own doctor now."

"Would you be more comfortable at home?" he asked me directly, Zelda laying in her plastic bin across the room.

"Yes," I said, thinking about home as though I hadn't been there in months. It had barely been twenty-four hours since we left, not even twelve since the birth.

What I should have thought or said to my doctor or to Josh was, "What equals comfort right now? What is best for us?" Walking was painful, and our house had two narrow, steep flights of stairs. There at the hospital, meals were delivered three times a day, someone came and gave me my medicine when it was time, and, if I needed, I could call a nurse to help me with the baby. I hadn't sent Zelda off to the nursery yet, but I knew that it was there. But I wanted so badly to go home that I didn't think about any of this. Like a child, I wanted what I wanted.

This was partly because I am a homebody. Josh loves hotels and often talks about how he would prefer to live in one. I prefer—need, actually—to be surrounded by my stuff. My books and my papers, my pillows and my bed. I sleep well only in a room that smells like me, and I think well only in my own office. I just wanted, longed, to be home.

But it was also, I see now, out of fear: this was my first-ever hospital stay. I simply wanted to go home. In fact, I felt the weight of my own childishness over and over those first few hormonal days. I wanted things. I wanted.

But now, I was a mother. I didn't yet know that soon I

would gladly saw off my own head with a butter knife to save my daughter's life, that my own wants would subside, seem to be deleted almost from my mind. I was in a kind of limbo state between adult human woman and mother. I inhabited in that hospital a competing sense of self, no place or time, nothing pressing from life back home that couldn't wait, but I was so excited to get back there.

I didn't know that my old home was gone, that I would never get it back, that it had been replaced. That the same old rooms would suddenly seem different on a molecular level. That the light would hit the furniture in a way I'd never seen before, that I would be up at hours I had never been awake at. That I would learn how to avoid a creaking step, how to walk as if on pillows so as not to make a sound. That I would sleep lightly instead of as if I were dead, how I'd slept my whole life up until now. Everything was different: not just me but the house, the dog, my husband. My books would sit on shelves unread for months; my former life was gone. I would not get a haircut or a pedicure for months. Everything was different; not worse, nor even better, just different.

But I didn't know that yet.

In the hospital, in the twenty-four hours after my daughter was born, I knew only my base impulses and desires. I had to get this newborn to feed, shoving my breast un-helpfully into her mouth. I wanted food. I had to have a bowel movement before I could leave. I had to get up and walk. I wanted a shower. Our daughter had to make wet diapers, she had to latch, she also had to poop. Everything was direct and simple, bodily and earthly. I texted friends and family, but no communications had any weight. Nothing mattered outside that room. That was clear, and the needs were pressing but so simple and direct. I had barely packed anything, and when people offered to bring me things I might need, I could not remember what I owned or even if owning things mattered. It was a Zen kind of feeling, which, when writing about it, sounds almost like apathy. Teetering on the edge of an ending and a beginning is a certain kind of not caring, really. What was next? Who cares.

I wanted to lose the water weight while I sat on the couch watching TV and eating takeout food like the old days. I couldn't think beyond those basic needs. I tried not to laugh because of the wound in my abdomen that I was still too scared to look at.

I hadn't given up my old life completely yet. That would take a few weeks to accomplish. For now, Josh and I were in a weird fog, and there was only one thing, besides the presence of Zelda, that forced me to admit that things had changed irrevocably.

I wanted my mother. On this, my first real day feeling like an adult after years of what now clearly seemed to have been "faking it," I wanted my mother there. Not for guidance or even support, but simply for her to be there. A model to look at, my mother, of someone who had successfully transitioned so early in life from a woman into a mother. A woman who, it seemed to me, had done so quite easily. A very normal but impossible wish. Becoming a mother had reduced me to a child instantly.

CHAPTER 3

• • •

My parents got married when they were very young, but they weren't unique in that: growing up, most of my friends' parents were young, too. This was something I thought of very much as I began my journey with Josh as the parents of a newborn. My parents were so young when they started having kids that I constantly compared myself to them. My mother would have been sixty-one years old when her granddaughter was born. That's so young. When I'm sixty-one years old, Zelda will only be twenty-four.

I guess I worried a little that I wouldn't have the same energy that my parents had had for us when we were kids. It wasn't that I felt old; I didn't. But having my daughter made me remember so many things about my own early childhood that I'd never thought about, couldn't have thought about, in the way I saw them now, as a mother.

For the first few years of my life, my parents lived in a small town surrounded by other people who were family: my great-uncle and great-aunt and two of my father's first cousins lived in houses up and down a small street filled with small houses. Because my parents were so young, so too were my grandparents, all four of them.

My mother and father grew up a few miles from each other and went to the same high school. My father was just about two years older than my mother. Not until they were in college, both of them going to Catholic schools in Erie, Pennsylvania, did they meet. Soon after my father graduated, our family began. So my grandparents were young, but they were also close geographically to us and to each other. This meant that family events were often large because they encompassed all of us, with cousins mostly nearby. My parents each had just one sibling, but the extended families were big and loud and always around.

My mother was—unlike me, her only daughter—chatty and outgoing, sunny and warm. I've struggled my whole life to make small talk. Like my father and many of the people on his side of the family, we sometimes are at a loss for words. Josh always remarks at how bad I am at even pretending to be having a good time in large groups of people, but as a child I don't remember that feeling as much. Children are often generously given space to be simply themselves, before adulthood begs us to behave in ways that make those around us more comfortable.

But my mother never struggled to fill air space. Deep in the furthest recesses of my memory I can recall her talking on the phone, talking all morning to my grandmothers and friends and cousins, just chatting away.

My parents often hosted the holidays, and my mother was, unlike her own mom, a great cook. I don't know where she picked it up, though I do remember her always sharing recipes with my grandma Elly, her mother-in-law. They were close too, and long after my mother was dead, my grandma Elly loved to tell stories about how she and my mother got along, talking and cooking and laughing.

There was never silence in our house; there were too many of us for that. I often wished, even when I was four or five, that things were quieter. Once my mother told me she'd woken up in the middle of the night to find me alone in a room, all the lights on, doing jigsaw puzzles. "I needed some quiet," I told her. I shared a bedroom first with my two brothers and, once my youngest brother, John, was born, we moved to a larger house, and I shared just with him, the baby. I loved having a baby in my room, at five or six years old, and betrayed no hint of my adult ambivalence about kids to come.

In that smaller house, where we lived when my brother Daniel was born right after me, my mother told me that sometimes, when he was sleeping in his bassinet in my parents' room, I would silently, quietly creep in and just stand there watching him. I could barely talk, but once, when my mother came in and found me there, I said, "Shhhhhh . . . baby sleeping." I loved my baby dolls as Zelda would eventually love hers, with a fervor that means she can now change a diaper faster than I can. I used to watch her on the baby monitor, early in the morning, awake and sitting up in the dark, staring up at the ceiling as she silently changed her baby's diaper over and over, practicing, a neat little stack of used diapers bundled next to her. But the arrival of Daniel, and later John, meant that I no longer needed to care for baby dolls: I had real-life specimens.

Just before we moved to the larger house, and just before John was born, my father found out that he had cancer. He was twenty-eight years old, and my parents had three kids. It was melanoma, the bad kind. As children, we were mostly sheltered from the realities of this, that my parents and grandparents thought that he might die, which they did think. Only later did my mother tell me, as a preteen in one of our long conversations about the past, how serious it had been, that they'd thought he might not survive. "Your grandmother came to the hospital once with her dress on inside out; everyone was a mess," she said. She was so candid with me, even as a kid. I was her friend and sounding board, in addition to being her daughter. "But," I said, remembering that period, "that's so strange. To me, that was one of the best times, because he was home for so long." My father hadn't worked for a while after his surgery. He'd spent a lot of time in bed in their darkened room. To me, it was great because he was just around all the time.

That larger house had a giant yard and a creek and woods behind it, and my brothers and I often spent the hours before I was in school yet roaming around outside all day. In my mind it was idyllic and normal enough, but I was also fairly rough around the edges, I think. My mother was always careful to dress me very well, but I had scrapes and bruises all over me from days spent climbing trees and building forts. I didn't have many friends of my own yet, just my brothers. I was surrounded by boys.

My mother stayed home with us, and I was so close in age to my brother Daniel, who was just sixteen months younger than me, that most of my first memories are of babies: him, then John, who was four years younger than me. My father worked a lot, as fathers often do. But we were surrounded by family on the weekends and neighborhood friends and mothers during the week.

I didn't go to kindergarten, so I stayed home with my
mother until I went to first grade, at the nearby Catholic
school. I remember her walking me out to the bus that first
day, me in a little jumper with pigtails and her kneeling down
in front of me. She had a cigarette in her left hand. Back then,
as I remember it, every parent smoked. My mother held my
hand—my brother David went to the same school, and he was
there off to the side—and we walked down our long driveway
to the road. He seemed so much older than me, a fifth grader.
I was excited to be starting school, to learn how to really read,
where then I just knew some words in the books I tried to
parse. I could write my name; my mother, who had studied
childhood education for her two years of college and had
wanted to be a teacher, had taught me how to write.

"You're going to be fine," she said.

I didn't feel afraid to leave her or to go off to school on my
own. I would quickly grow to love my class, my teacher, the
little dark hallway that led from the school of just fifty or
sixty students to the beautiful church. I wanted to go. I was
ready to go.

But I felt, even then at six, that my mother wanted me to
want to stay home. She had tears in her eyes as she knelt in
front of me.

I couldn't think of anything to say to reassure her or make
her feel what I felt she wanted from me. I thought she wanted
to hear me say that I would rather stay home, but that wasn't
true. She'd formed me already into a little independent
person, and there I was, happy to leave her. She still had
Daniel and John at home, of course, and what's striking in
hindsight more than anything else are my tiny feelings of ob-
ligation to her. Even that young, I felt that in some way she

needed me more than I needed her. But maybe that was only in my six-year-old imagination.

My mother had taught me, so young, to be happy left to myself. I listened to my records and looked at books alone in my room, colored pictures happily. My parents were strict: we didn't watch a lot of TV, and we did what we were told.

One night, probably around the same time as I entered first grade, I made what I recall as my first act of rebellion against my parents. At dinner, the six of us sat there talking at the dining room table. At our house, you didn't question what was for dinner; you simply ate what was on offer. This was mostly for convenience: you can't cater to the whims of six people, four of whom are little kids. So we dutifully ate what was provided.

On the night in question, my mother made pea soup. It was the kind of pea soup that was pork based, little bits of ham floating among the muck. I realized as I sat there, staring at it, that I hated pea soup. I tried to eat it but simply couldn't muster the enthusiasm required for it.

"I don't want this," I said.

My parents looked over at me.

My little brother Dan echoed me. "Me neither." I could be ushering in a full-scale mutiny, my parents probably realized.

"You need to eat," my father said. He was tough and quiet, affectionate, but he always stuck to his word. I carried a normal sense of awe and fear a girl my age had for her father. I adored him but didn't fuck with him. Ever. He never hit me or even raised his voice very often, but when he did yell, it was loud and scary. I don't remember my parents fighting back then. I had no reason to fear him, but I did.

"I'm not eating this; it's gross," I said.

My father put down his spoon and sat there for a second, planning his response.

"Your mother made this; it's delicious. Please eat. That's enough," he said.

I could have pretended to eat. I could have slipped through the cracks with all the other people at the table. I could have said nothing. But I wanted to see where this could go.

"No."

Everyone else was finishing up. David, I could see by the looks he was shooting me, thought I was incredibly dumb to bother with any of this. Daniel sat beside me, not eating either but no longer repeating whatever I said. My mother stood up and started clearing the bowls away. She reached over my shoulder to take mine.

"Leave it," my father said. "She can sit there until she finishes."

And so I sat. I sat for what seemed like hours but was probably twenty minutes. It got dark outside, the sun went down, my brothers were in the other room watching TV. I sat there, waiting for something to happen. For someone to release me from the agony and boredom of simply sitting there, a now-cold bowl of soup in front of me.

My mother came in from the kitchen, having finished washing the dishes. My father appeared. She took the bowl and walked into the kitchen without saying anything to either of us.

"You can go to bed now," he said.

I went to my room and cried myself to sleep, still dressed in my clothes from the day. An hour or so later, my father woke me up. He was sitting on my bed.

"I'm sorry," I said.

He picked me up and carried me downstairs, where my mother and David were still awake, watching television.

I don't know if this was the same night, but in my memory, it was: the night that we watched, together in our family room, the Motown twenty-fifth-anniversary special. The first time I remember seeing Michael Jackson perform live. My parents loved music, and they sat there with us, watching this insane genius sing "Billie Jean" and moonwalk across the stage. My parents were like that, then: our minor misbehavior, to the extent that it happened, was silently passed over. The subtext was clear. You learned the lesson—don't do it again—but nobody made you feel too badly about yourself in the process, either.

Home was, for all of my first six or seven years on planet Earth, warm and loud, and the doors were always open, usually literally. The sound of the screen door banging open and shut as kids or neighbors or family streamed in is baked into my memory: I remember specific screen doors, the metal ones of the two houses, the wooden ones at my grandma Elly's, where the policy was the same, everybody welcome.

Home was warm and normal until it wasn't, and there weren't, in my memory, any warning signs of the change, which came swiftly and abruptly. I'm sure my parents struggled and that they learned fitfully how to manage four young children, their finances, all the things that come with having a family. I wasn't ever naive or unaware, though I was a very small child at one point. Often I find myself in disagreement with anyone who believes that children are unaware of the serious, adult problems going on around them. I was always, to my mind, sensitive to the adults in my midst. And though I see now with Zelda how the nuance of an argument may be lost on her, it's also very true that she senses the broad strokes and tone of a serious discussion. Any time Josh and I have argued around her, I have felt her tense up and close down into her mind. She listens and waits, the way I myself listened and waited.

My mother was in lots of ways a very typical late 1970s or early 1980s stay-at-home mother. She paid lots of attention to us, but we also roamed on our own in little groups as she cooked and cleaned and did laundry, soap operas sometimes playing in the living room in the background. She was laid-back and left us to our own devices a lot, not out of neglect but simply out of the necessity of running a big household.

◆　◆　◆

Josh and I couldn't have gone into our new life as parents more differently. We were older, which meant that Zelda's grandparents were older, too. We were both by nature loners without many close friends. The friends we did have were not parents themselves. We lived in Brooklyn, hundreds of miles away from our immediate families. We both worked a lot, and I had no intention—none—of staying home with Zelda for longer than the twelve weeks allotted to me by my job.

In Brooklyn, I knew no other stay-at-home mothers. I didn't consider myself a stay-at-home mother; my sojourn home with my daughter was to be just that twelve weeks, and yet, I almost immediately had many of the problems of any stay-at-home mother: I needed some other stay-at-home mom friends. I was lonely. Daytime television sucked. The baby was boring. Days were long.

We thought, in a wrongheaded but probably unavoidable,

nearly universal manner of first-time parents, that Zelda would slide right into our old lives, causing minor disruption and increasing photo ops, but we did not suspect that she would devour, overnight, our way of living.

Josh and I were on our own and uninformed about the ways of modern parenting. If we needed help, we'd have to hire it. I've never excelled at asking for help, and there, in the first few days at home with Zelda, was no different. I'd blindly gone through pregnancy assuming I could simply pile on the extra duties of motherhood to my already overflowing work and home stack. I'd managed our household for years. I'd handled our finances and taxes; all of that was my domain. Though I had lots of ideas about "equal parenting" based on feminism and shit, and though I was totally uninformed about the actual real labor involved in taking care of a baby, I carried few illusions about who would do most of the work: I knew that it would probably be me. I knew it would be me because I wanted it to be me. I like being capable and busy and in charge. I knew that I would suck up extra work in the family and with Zelda because I wanted to do things my way. I looked forward to this.

Those first few weeks at home were an insane mixture of joy tempered with the realities of a newborn. Big cities are weirdly isolating places to have children, simply because most of us living in them aren't from there, so when we do have kids, the rest of our family—parents, siblings, cousins—aren't around to fill up those long and somewhat lazy hours.

I'd made a conscious decision to leave my familiar sur-roundings of family and friends behind, to move a six-hour drive away from them, as had my husband. We didn't think about what it would be like when we had kids. Does anyone?

In the early days of Zelda's life, it was the three of us—me, her, and Josh—most of the time on the weekends, with a smaller circle of friends, none of whom had kids, who would stop over occasionally for a visit.

During the weekday hours, though, almost no one was around. Josh went back to work one week after Zelda was born, though he'd intended to stay home longer, called back by something that seemed to us at the time worthy of his return. It wasn't ideal for any of us, and we hadn't planned it that way, but that was what happened. We, Zelda and I, were on our own. A lot.

I want to tell you that this transition was easy for me, but it wasn't. I didn't know, going into motherhood, that newborn babies didn't really sleep. I assumed that they slept a lot, and though they sort of do, I didn't know what constituted sleep and what was awake. She was noisy and greedy and seemed unhappy in her new life a lot. Though it was clear from the get-go that Zelda was a "good baby," any baby is rough on the uninitiated. And I, so used to living in my head and having hours of time to myself to think and daydream and cook elaborate meals, was in for a wake-up call. And the first few weeks with Zelda were all about sleep—or a lack of it, I guess. All three of us were hampered by exhaustion.

But I need to say that part of the reason the transition was so hard for me was that I felt an intense amount of pressure to "do" motherhood well. I wanted to do it well, I was desperate to be a devoted and caring and attentive mother from the start. I am naturally competitive with myself, and I love to multitask. I wanted to be a great mother but also to manage all the things I'd managed before: the house, our money, my career. I'd waited quite a long time to have children, and so when she arrived, I assumed my daughter would necessarily be the focus of my efforts moving forward. And though in the first months I did not yet feel the pull of going back to work, of my career and my own projects, I *did* feel, keenly and selfishly, the loss of personal time. The loss of time to be just alone with myself. She was always there. We didn't have time apart. I hadn't thought about this in advance. And I didn't know, couldn't know, how hard it actually is to be a parent. How much labor it is, emotionally, physically, and mentally. And I began, very quickly, to see that having a career and a well-loved daughter and an orderly house was not simply a matter of me *wanting* it badly enough. I began to suspect that I would run myself ragged, possibly for the rest of my life. But still, I was up for it most days.

While Josh was exhausted at work, I was exhausted at home with a baby who didn't ever seem fully awake or fully asleep. She existed in some middling state where I could barely put her down for fear that she would start crying. She didn't cry much, to be fair to her: she was pretty lovely from the start, like I said. But my options often seemed limited to simply letting her sleep on my chest or never at all. At night, it was worse.

I remember one desolate Sunday morning when Zelda was just two weeks old, where no one had slept and when Josh and I had argued, at 4:45 a.m., over who would "get up for the day" with the baby. I had lost. I usually did, simply because Josh had to be "presentable," he had "a real job." I say these things in quotation marks not because his words were untrue. They were absolutely true. It's impossible to go to a job and seem even seminormal on the amount of sleep that he and I were getting. But, at the same time, hearing him say it to me, in the state that I was in, made me want to spit fire. I'd been home for only two weeks and already I couldn't conceive of the world outside my house. I was hopelessly self-involved and didn't think beyond a few hours ahead of myself.

That Sunday morning, I reached a crisis point. I couldn't keep not sleeping at night only to have to be conscious during the day, too. My incision still hurt when I laughed (which was sort of more often than I'm making it sound like here, right now), and walking up and down the stairs was terrifying. During the day I kept the baby on the first floor with me all day, jetting up the stairs as fast as my still-swollen feet could carry me only to go to the bathroom while she slept in a basket on the couch, our dog, Penny, standing guard.

I emailed a friend of mine who had told me that when he and his wife had twins, they'd hired a baby nurse. I only vaguely knew what a baby nurse was, but in that moment of the email, so tired and overwhelmed as I was, I knew simply that I wanted one. I needed one. Three scattered emails back and forth and I was on the phone with a woman who said she could come that evening. She would stay, she said, from 8:00 p.m. until 7:00 a.m. I would, in those hours, do nothing. Do whatever I wanted. Sleep. Eat. I didn't know.

At 8:00 that night, Monica showed up at my door. We were in the middle of blundering through "bath time," which was still terrifying and seemingly full of danger. She took Zelda from me and, in a matter of less than five minutes, had expertly cleaned and toweled off her body. "See, like this," she said, as Josh and I stood behind her, marveling. "The baby gets cold very fast, so the bath should only take two minutes," she said.

We followed her into Zelda's bedroom, and I showed her

where everything that they could possibly need was in the tiny space. She put Zelda into her little pajamas, and I handed her a bottle. "Good night," she said. "Don't worry."

"She doesn't sleep much," I said.

"But you should," she said.

I went upstairs and laid across my bed. I burst into tears. After ten minutes, I crawled under the covers, fully clothed, and fell asleep. I didn't wake up until the next morning at 7:15, when Josh shook me to let me know that the nurse was ready to leave.

"She slept four and a half hours straight," Monica told me as she bundled herself up to go out into the bitter Brooklyn cold. "I'll see you tonight."

Monica came back on and off for two weeks, just so that we could get some sleep, so that I could recover from surgery and be present with Zelda during the long, twelve-hour days, and so that Josh could manage better at work. It was a great decision and a good lesson for me: asking for help is often the greatest thing a mother can do.

I've wished so many times for family to be closer since we became parents, especially when Zelda's grandparents come to visit. Each of the four of them (my father remarried the same year that Josh and I got married) loves her so much, and she them. I had very close and special relationships growing up with my own grandparents, and I want that for her, too.

But we don't have, mostly because of proximity, the same relationship with our parents, Zelda's grandparents, as my parents had with theirs. Geographical distance means long-planned trips to visit are a big deal, not thrown together at the last minute. And of course, grandparents are, for us, never a last-minute babysitter option. Where my parents had access to their own parents for help—I remember my grandmother always came along on shopping trips and to doctor's appointments, and I realize now that it was probably because a second set of hands was really helpful—Josh and I hire helpers: we find babysitters and housekeepers and try to manage the best we can mostly on our own. There are upsides to isolation, but only when I became a parent did I realize how much easier family life could be if only there were more, well, *family* around, and how important it is for Zelda to be close to her aunts and uncles and grandparents.

CHAPTER 4

• • •

've learned a lot from Zelda. There's been a lot of nuts-
and-bolts acquiring of skills over the past few years. The
early days of complete cluelessness died extremely hard and
really fast. I am now officially "good with babies and children."
I know how to talk to them and keep them calm, how to be
firm without being mean. I can stay patient in the face of the
great annoyance of small children. I've discovered that even
young babies can learn by example and that children always
do. But Zelda has taught me by example, too.

She was always outgoing and social, even as an infant,
often smiling and, once she learned to wave, waving at
strangers. My mother's alcoholism had forced me to be pro-
tective and reserved, suspicious of common, everyday interactions with neighbors and mailmen. I kept secrets and
information to myself; often I pulled away from my closest
friends, even when I was very young. There were always so
many things I couldn't tell. Zelda's natural inclination was to
be open and to greet everyone. She is, like my mother was (and
like her father), a friend-maker: talk comes fast and easy to her.

But more than that, being a mother was isolating in a way

in which I did not expect. I didn't expect to want to talk to other people going through the same thing as me. I'd gone through plenty of serious experiences in my life before. I'd had friends die, I'd dealt with my mother's alcoholism and her death, and I'd mostly gone through those things with only Josh and my closest family to support me. I didn't generally reach out to random people. But becoming a mother broke me open: I wanted to talk about the experience of motherhood and about my life as it was now. About how hard the transition was.

But I also just wanted some company in those long days.

"My mother is dead" is a terrible icebreaker, but, in the months after Zelda was born, I was pretty raw most of the time. And when I said it to a new mother I'd just met named Kim, it felt perfectly natural, the words tumbling out of my mouth easily and without tears or doubt. I knew that it would lead to other conversations, that it meant a lot of explanation, a narrative. I knew that it would burden our friendship and possibly tie us together in ways that I often avoided with other people. But it felt, like I said, perfectly natural. I was open and ready to tell the story. And I'd met Kim in an unlikely place: a meet-up of new mothers, with infants all about the same age as Zelda. Driven by something like desperation, I reached out to a random group of people. And I met Kim.

The first meet-up that Zelda and I went to was painful for me: it was in a park, a twenty-minute walk from our house. I walked with her strapped to my chest in a baby carrier, pushing the empty stroller in case she changed her mind about where she was most comfortable. She burped and spit up a little, drool rolling down between my breasts and, disgustingly, into my belly button. I noticed I hadn't charged my phone before we left the house, so I wouldn't even have that crutch if the experience was really grim: we were on our own. It was spring, and although it wasn't too cold anymore, venturing out still felt new and terrifying but, at least, exciting. The point of the meet-up, I see now at least for myself, was simply to motivate me to leave the house.

The group of women I met was about what I expected. They were mostly young, straight, and white. They were artists and writers, and one worked all over the world researching HIV. They were uniformly smart, well educated. Most of them were first-time mothers. We had things in common, to be sure: we were all exhausted, and we were all struggling with sleeping, breast-feeding, the basics, even a few months in. Some struggled more than others: I was well on my way to solving some of my problems, since I was sleep training and supplementing with formula; others seemed racked with guilt at the thought of such things. It was a judgment-free space, but I felt that judgment was on the tips of all our tongues. I wasn't the only one who was raw, of course.

Still, it was good to see the babies there together on blankets in a park on a nice day. And though it pained me to admit it, I needed this, and I went home that day with a very slight spring in my step and something even more important.

"I think I made a friend today," I said when Josh came home.

"That's weird," he joked.

"I'm not sure yet, really. We'll see." I was cautiously optimistic, and only time would tell.

But the next week there was another meet-up, this time in the backroom event space of a local baby store. This time, the babies could really just roll around however; we didn't need to worry about them banging into bugs or twigs. Well, except that my baby, my Zelda, she didn't really roll over yet. Some of the babies who were even younger were already rolling, but not my girl. She was seemingly content to stay pretty much wherever I set her down.

Kim was there again, and her daughter, Amy, who was just one day older than Zelda, wasn't rolling over yet either, though she was closer to doing so than Zelda.

My memory of this day is vital to my life as a mother. It's not that I'm so socially awkward that I can't make friends. But wanting a friend who was specifically a "mom" at what seemed to me like the most vulnerable time in my life felt, well, a little undignified. But that raw vulnerability—surely a liability in many situations—also made me open to talking, and to listening, to someone completely new.

We had a lot in common. In fact, every time that we talked—and we were soon trading text messages and meeting almost daily for little jaunts around the neighborhood with our strollers—we found that we had more to say. We'd both had C-sections; we were both sleep training. We came from similar family backgrounds. We were both musicians in a previous iteration. And we both admitted, at least to each other, that sometimes being a mother seemed like too much.

"I wonder if I made a huge mistake," I said to her one time.

"I think I'm good with the one," she said to me another. I had found a kindred spirit. And I knew it.

In the hours we spent together, I told Kim pretty much everything I had to tell. I hadn't written in months, and I craved a connection not just about the baby but about my whole life. I hadn't felt alone in quite this way in so long—

usually, being alone was a positive thing for me; left with my thoughts I felt quite at home. But now was different.

It was simple for me, in some ways, to tell Kim about my mother. The rawness of my birth experience backed me up, cut me open, but it also made everything that had happened before seem pale and incapable of hurting me. I saw, as I told Kim what I had to tell her, that in a lot of ways, I couldn't be hurt by it anymore.

This is the essence of true friendship. I lived as a friend to Emily for a very long time before I could utter the words "my mother is a drunk" to her. She must have known for years, and yet I couldn't say them aloud. But Kim would never know my mother. I could divulge the unvarnished truth about her, and Kim could judge my mother however she did, and nothing would come of it. Being an adult means no longer having your identity partly or even mostly determined by your background. My mother being an alcoholic didn't mean that there was something wrong with me.

I had known this fact for a pretty long time by the spring of 2014, when I met Kim, when we rolled our strollers double-wide up and down the many sidewalks of Greenpoint. It made saying the words easier but no less powerful. I folded the truth of my upbringing into my identity in a way that said, "Here, this is who I am. I'm okay." Kim was the first person I'd really become fully, socially friends with in the years since my mother died. It mattered that she was "my" friend, not "our" friend: she had never met Josh. I told her whatever I wanted to tell her. We complained about our spouses as spouses, as fathers, at a time when venting was crucial. We vented and, for me at least, I gained strength in representing myself in a way that was both honest and on my terms.

"My mother isn't alive anymore," I said, one bright afternoon. It was a beginning.

And what I revealed there, in those first few months of motherhood, what I came to terms with, was the fact that motherhood was not going to be as easy for me as I had imagined. I was already aware of this just a few days after my daughter was born. Already, I suspected that my dreams of writing at my computer with a baby on the blanket in my office beside me might have been a little optimistic. I wasn't sure what the future held, and, for the first time in my life, for the first time since childhood, I felt open to the possibilities of female friendship as a way to help me figure it out.

But my first friend was Emily. After spending much of my young life surrounded primarily by my brothers, I met Emily the first day of second grade. That summer we had moved an hour away to a suburb of Pittsburgh that was quite different from where we had been before. More than the small-town, very middle-class, Polish Catholic environment where family was literally on the same street on which I lived, our move to McMurray changed everything for us.

This was also when I realized that my mother had a problem, or when it became impossible for her to hide it from me. I think my mother started drinking at home during the day sometimes when we were all at school. I think she must have had some kind of pre–empty-nest syndrome; I'm not sure if there's a name for it. Her children were still a huge responsibility, a massive amount of day-to-day work and care, but she also suddenly, once my youngest brother went to kindergarten the year after we moved, had a massive block of hours at home alone. Time she had never had in her life because, of course, my mother had gone straight from living in a dorm room with friends to being married with children. She'd never been left to herself for hours on end. Unlike me, she may not have known what to do with all that time. My mother made friends easily, and our neighborhood was filled with other families with kids about our ages, so she wasn't isolated, but I sensed eventually that she wasn't at ease in the same way she had been in our old house, in our old neighborhood. Our grandparents were suddenly farther away, and though her children were a lot older than Zelda is now, I see how this must have felt for her: a lot like what it felt like for Josh and me in Brooklyn at first, with not much family around and no other parent friends.

But I didn't sense right away that the move, which meant for me a blossoming circle of friends, meant for my mother a new isolation where she was surrounded by more upper-middle-class women who gardened and got their nails done. For me, the move meant a new house that was larger. For the first time in my life I got to have my own bedroom away from my increasingly annoying brothers. I got to go to a new school that I loved. I got to go to dance classes with my friends. Sometimes my mother was a darker version of herself, but mostly she was still the mother I knew and loved. And I met Emily.

Emily had moved from Ohio the same summer, so we were both new to our second-grade class in a room of kids who had mostly been together for a few years of school. We lived just a mile apart from each other.

Emily and I latched onto each other, and it was a relationship that stuck through the rest of our school days together. We shared many things in common, but, in the early days, we mostly liked to play with Emily's vast Barbie doll collection and listen to Madonna.

Emily and I soon became the kind of friends who shared everything. But kids keep secrets, and I kept to myself my growing sense was that something was wrong with my mother. She seemed suddenly less happy and less present. I don't know when Emily figured out that my mother was an alcoholic, because we didn't talk about it until I was a teenager. I hid this from her reflexively: it was something we shouldn't and didn't talk about. I didn't make a conscious choice to not talk about this with her; it simply didn't really occur to me.

Emily was, at eight years old, a lot different than me. She was funny, like her mother, but she was also more assertive and seemed to always know what she wanted from life. She was probably less burdened inside than me. She certainly had better school attendance She was more active, where I was more reserved and unsure, quiet and, well, if not laid-back, certainly "retiring." I far preferred reading to playing outside.

And even though I wanted to spend all my time outside of school with Emily, already I sometimes craved isolation. By third grade I was keeping a secret diary. I'd love to be able to say that I started my writing career honestly, but I didn't. I had an eye to a future reader, one to whom being honest about my worries, and my beloved mother, was inconceivable. I even lied to my diary.

In fact, I'm cringing now as I write about this. It isn't easy to explain that someone you love so desperately is so complicated. I'm almost forty. It easily took me until I was thirty to be fully proud of my mother, blemishes and all. This is hard for any person to master, to accept and love people as they are rather than how we wish they could be, but for me, I can't help but blame the alcoholism in particular. I was defensive of her above all else.

And so it was that sometimes I pulled away into myself, even from my best friend, even that young. There were many things I couldn't tell her. We talked until all hours of the night in my bed or hers, about our hopes for the future, about moving to New York to become advertising executives (we watched a lot of soap operas after school), about our mutual fear of our houses burning down. We shared many things, almost everything. But not quite.

Soon after we met, Emily's parents separated and her father moved out, leaving her mother with their three daughters. That seemed inconceivable to me, my father leaving, and I know that it wasn't easy for her. And yet, still, I was jealous of her. I knew with all my being that *her* mother was, for lack of a better word, consistent. She didn't occasionally morph into a completely different person who didn't care or hated her. Emily had her secrets, her private griefs; I'm sure of that now as an adult. But what alcoholism does to you when you experience it as a child is that it makes you crave simple normalcy above all else. I didn't want more money or better clothes or toys or anything else a kid can want. I just spent all my spare time at home looking, like a detective, for signs that things were "okay."

One thing my increasingly drunk mother did really early on was stop showing up. At first, I thought she had just forgotten me. Which, on the one hand, she had. But on the other, she was drunk, which I know now means that the forgetting was a symptom, not the reason: she forgot because she was drunk, not because she disliked me.

This dissonance—that my sober mother loved me very much, that she braided my hair and sang to me, bought me little matching jumpers and sock sets, and made sure I was inoculated and had a lunch packed with little love notes in pen on the napkin tucked inside but then forgot to even bother picking me up occasionally, with barely a nod in my direction in apology after the fact—that I began to experience, where suddenly I wasn't first on her list but now seemed last, was quite confusing. Years later, it was still hurtful, and even now as I sit here typing I feel overwhelming sadness for the eight-year-old me, with no front teeth and bad eyesight, waiting at school after a voice lesson or a dance class, all the other kids filing out with their mothers, me just standing there, getting more nervous by the second. But then, I didn't feel hurt yet. I was too confused to take it personally. I felt nervous, and it was the nervousness that I would also keep for years to come.

But that lack of reliability was the first thing I remember about her drunkenness, beyond the drunkenness.

Mostly, my mother drank when I was in bed and my father was working late or wasn't home. So I didn't actually experience my drunk mother right off the bat too much. I would experience the very beginning of it, at the end of the school day when she was just getting rolling, or I would experience the tail end of it, when she seemed groggy or out of sorts the next morning. Those times I woke up and the usual morning routine was absent; no one was making breakfast. Sometimes, I learned, there were no lunches packed for school. That's how I experienced my mother's drinking at the start, mostly. There were a few encounters of her actively drinking, but in the beginning it was just that little things were off.

I would get up to go to the bathroom or get a drink of water, and though it seemed very late, instead of the house being quiet, there were the unmistakable sounds of life: creaking floorboards, a closing cupboard. My mother would be down the hall, in the kitchen, on the phone. The phone cord was a mile long, and she paced through the kitchen and living room, into the hallway where most of the bedrooms were. We lived in a one-story ranch house with a vast basement. In that vast basement was my two younger brothers' bedroom, a family room, a playroom, the laundry room. It was mostly unfinished and somehow both scary and attractive to me. That basement is where I began writing, sitting at a little antique school desk, the kind with the arm that swings around from the left side, immovable, for a right-handed person. I sat in and used that desk from the time I was five until I left home at eighteen. Over the holiday last year, I had my father pull it out of storage and bring it to my house, where we plunked it down in Zelda's playroom. I still fit in it; I can squeeze my body tightly in, and it feels right. Zelda is left-handed, so it's never going to be her favorite desk, but it's hers anyway.

The sound of my mother's drunk voice talking into the telephone will never fade. Hearing one side of a conversation is so odd to begin with; it's like eavesdropping, but the picture painted seems much more mysterious than if you could hear the other person. It had to be after 10:00, 11:00 at night. Who was she talking to? I knew from my time before going to school that my mother spent hours during the day on the phone with my grandmothers, with neighbors. She was a talkative, outgoing, and friendly person. She smoked, she paced, and she talked. If there wasn't someone sitting in the kitchen at the table with her, she was usually on the phone. The phone was a big deal in the '80s.

During the day, she would trample around the kitchen, making dinner or folding clothes, talking on the phone. But at night, she was usually sitting instead of pacing or multi-tasking. At night, she was always smoking. And the sound of her voice was different. As different as it could be from her day voice. And this is how I learned my one adult strategy for dealing with my mother: no matter what, under no circum-stances would I answer the phone after 5:00 p.m. As a teenager newly moved out on my own and later as an adult, any breaking of this rule always resulted in a horrible conver-sation that I regretted and she forgot. My husband's father always said, "Nothing good happens after one a.m." Well, with my mother that was true, except it was 5:00 p.m. You could hear in her voice the moment she started drinking, and in fact, in later years, I sometimes took a call at a safe time— say 4:30 p.m., right when she was leaving work, only to have the call drift into an unsafe, post–5:00 p.m. drinking time. I'd hear the beer can crack open, and within a few minutes her voice thickened and slowed. Within half an hour she was ar-gumentative or, worse, sad.

A full-on encounter with my drunk mother late at night was something I instinctively avoided. As a child, I was not yet a worthy adversary or sounding board for her. In fact, from about the age of eight to thirteen, when my mother drank, I became invisible. I had to graduate to teenager-dom in order to be interesting to her. In some ways, when I think back on it, though my teenage years were more explosive and harder, the childhood ones are so much lonelier, quieter, and sadder. So much more desolate.

Avoiding my drunk mother, staying quiet and in line, hoping not to incur notice or scrutiny: these things molded who I am today. I didn't argue then, and I didn't talk very much. But I was nervous and watchful, because, I see now, I didn't really trust adults. Because the one I was supposed to be able to trust the most, the one who I had *once* trusted the most, suddenly pulled the rug out from under me.

How had this happened? My mother didn't start out this way. The first seven years or so of my life seemed completely normal, if self-absorbed and contracted in my memory. But I have hundreds, thousands of glorious childhood memories stacked inside my brain, all weirdness-free.

After she was gone, after she had died, I became an investigator of her life for a few months. To the extent that I could stand it, I asked around: Had she always been this way? Were the signs always there? Was it just that I was too young to see them?

Yes and no.

As I said, my sense is that our move to McMurray hastened my mother's developing alcoholism. I don't remember her drinking before that, though I assume that she did sometimes, because that's what would have been normal. Nobody in my family drank to excess, but there was always beer around at family functions. But at first, all of this was vague and mysterious. I'd always been so close to my mother; I thought of her as a friend, as a person to whom I could tell absolutely anything, and so, when I realized for sure that she had a problem drinking around the time I was eight or so, the first person I shared this information with was her.

I knew that my mother was an alcoholic before I knew the word for it, and I guarded this knowledge as if it were my own secret, not hers. I was, as a sober person, even at the age of eight, better at hiding her alcoholism than she was, anyway. And she was pretty good for a while. This threw off the mother-child dynamic considerably, and I grew up to be a textbook adult child of an alcoholic. But we learned what alcoholism was at school, probably in third grade. This fact, the naming of the problem, worried me because it sounded very serious, but it also simplified my focus. And it was like the last piece in a jigsaw puzzle for me: this made sense. I felt relief as I worked this out, the fact that her personality changed sometimes, that she became less reliable. All of it made sense and helped me to organize my feelings around alcoholism as a disease rather than as simply something to hide and be embarrassed about.

Alcoholism teaches you to compartmentalize your relationships, and even though I was very young, I did this quickly. I didn't talk to my brothers about it very much. I didn't ask my father many questions. There were no group discussions. Ironically, the only person I could be fully honest with in this situation was my mother.

I think about those early confrontations with my mother now and I cringe, the idea of a small child coming to her and saying, "Here, I found the answer, I know what is wrong with you, and there is a solution." I felt, once I'd latched onto the concept of alcoholism, a great relief: here was a plan, with a fix. Just like me later as an adult, I spent a long time paralyzed by inertia and fear and anxiety, and then I latched onto a solution that spurred me to action. The path seemed clear. I only needed to confront my mother carefully and present her with my plan.

What I didn't know yet was how poorly that would go and how poorly it would always go. For all the lying-by-omission I learned to do for the outside world, my alcoholic mother honed techniques for evasion that I simply was never able to breach. I was at the beginning, not the end, of trying to mobilize and change her. And though I would feel nothing but defeat over and over, I still know today that it was better than to live without trying.

I told her that there was a cure for this! There was help for it; it was simple. "You're an alcoholic," I said to her, not yet nine years old, a little kid in pigtails. I didn't judge. I crawled beside her and hugged her. She assured me that she was fine, she reassured me that I was safe, that she loved me. And she ignored me.

Adult Children of Alcoholics, much like Al-Anon, describes the way that being parented by, or loved by, an alcoholic changes you. Most commonly, and what I found to be most true for myself, was the fact that I lost my own identity. I was always nervous; I dreaded and handled personal criticism very poorly; and more than anything else, I found it easier to focus on other people than to focus on myself. This part, what I think of as "the killer," is something I struggle with today: I can always find someone else to focus on rather than take care of myself or my own business. I was, in some ways, erased.

But before I became an adult child of an alcoholic, I was first and foremost the child of one. The only daughter of an alcoholic mother of four. I knew with most of my being what was wrong with her from about the third grade and was certain of it by the fifth. By then, I would have walked through a fire for her, and there was occasionally the sense that such a scenario might actually be necessary. This—the child willing to walk through the fire for the parent—is a classic hallmark of kids with alcoholic parents. Flipped roles, confused emotional responses: nearly all my feelings for my mother then and even many of them now can be explained by an entry-level rehab counselor as "part of this shit."

I think I probably knew that my mother drank too much, too often, even years before my father did, but I wasn't going to let him know it. I have always believed this because my mother eventually stopped drinking around my father at all; she hid her drinking from him but not from me. She either considered me too stupid to know what I was seeing, or knew that I would never tell on her. This is one of the most upsetting and manipulative parts of a relationship with an alcoholic parent: they use you and turn you, inadvertently, into their protector, a liar. I became secretive and guarded, not just around friends but even around my own immediate family. I could have resisted, I could have raised hell and told my father every time that she drank, but I just wanted peace and hoped that each time was the last.

All I wanted was for it to stop, for her to simply cease being what she was. I didn't have a full concept of alcoholism as a disease, and with a child's sad and frightening simplicity, I figured that she simply could stop if she wanted to. She probably could stop for me. Why would someone do something that they knew was bad for them, that made them different than their ideal self? Only a child would oversimplify this, only a child could see reality so clearly, as this is, honestly, the problem every alcoholic must face eventually:

the only solution is the simplest, hardest thing in the world. Stop.

I knew this so well and so fast and so completely. And yet I was so powerless. Little did I know how long I would remain powerless and how it would tear me apart, ruining relationships and holidays and life events, overshadowing, degrading. It added nothing, only taking away.

Little did I know that this would be the defining reality of my life: my mother was an alcoholic.

When I think back to these earliest days of recognizing that something about reality was off, that something was really wrong and that it wasn't about me, I see that I abruptly became aware that the world was full of secrets and full of lies. That adults lied, and that they presented things in different ways depending on the scenario or their moods. This terrified and confused me. Everything before had seemed so simple. What a short time for life to be simple. What a takeaway for a child to take away.

Years later, I look back at my attempts to reach out to my mother and my attempts to make friends, and I see that they were all in the shadows of my growing sense of my mother's disease. Her disease crippled my ability, even into adulthood, to be honest and open enough with people to make true connections. Only occasionally did I allow people into what I thought of as an elite circle of people who knew. With few exceptions, always in times of great personal tragedy, I guarded my mother's secret and more generally myself, as if I too carried some secret inside of me. Knowing that I did not, that I had no baggage or demons of my own, did me little good. It quickly became a reflex not to trust myself to be true with other people.

But Zelda changed all of that.

I know that I have Zelda to thank for my midlife burst of social activity. She, through sheer force of her existence but also through her sunny and able way, showed me that sometimes it's best to get to know people. Sometimes, it's best to reach out and share things. Sometimes, it's best to simply burst into tears when you're having a bad day. It's okay to cry in public. It's okay to tell someone you're in pain. I'd spent much of my childhood trying to be an adult. Now, I got to spend a small piece of my adulthood occasionally being exactly like a baby, my emotions sometimes overwhelming me, calling out to strangers and old friends. Helping random people on the street who'd dropped everything out of their purse or who simply looked lost. Zelda changed the way that I interacted with everyone.

CHAPTER 5

◆ ◆ ◆

Back when I was pregnant, way before we found out that the baby was sideways inside of me, and way, way before the preeclampsia, we toured the hospital where Zelda would be born. We, along with maybe ten other couples, took in the available options for the birth plan we would never make. We looked at hospital rooms; we learned about payment options. It seemed like a required waste of time, really. I have never liked being in hospitals. Until Zelda was born, I had never spent a night in one. I'd never had a broken bone or needed my appendix taken out.

For me, like many people, hospitals have almost always been for deaths. My grandparents, great-aunts and -uncles, my mother: they all ended their lives inside cramped hospital rooms. I don't avoid hospitals, because I know I can't avoid sickness and death, but I have never enjoyed being inside of them, and anytime I was in one, I wanted out of there; I couldn't breathe in there.

As we followed the other couples down the long Labor and Delivery hallway, one of the rooms was still covered in bloody bedclothes. An expectant father paced the hallway, texting on his phone. The air in the maternity ward was alive and terrifying. It was different than other hospitals I'd been in: here, life started rather than ended.

As we were leaving after our two-hour tour, waiting for the elevator to take us back to street level, a couple trundled through the hallway: the man was carrying a tiny infant car seat. I now knew what an infant car seat was because I'd just bought one a few weeks earlier. They were leaving the hospital, taking their just-born baby home, giggling all the way out the door.

Josh and I exchanged little glances nervously between ourselves—the couple were in their own universe. "They seemed like they were stealing the baby," I said with a laugh. And they did: What right did they have to take that tiny little sleeping thing, just a few pounds, out the door? What were their qualifications? Surely I would be more ready than that.

But I wasn't. The early days were awash in simple concerns: feeding and sleeping. Though I often approached life ready and waiting with an answer for everything, I found myself devoid of knowledge at home with a newborn, unprepared to answer even basic questions. "Is she tired?" Don't know. "Is that rash normal?" Can't say. We'd had Monica for a few weeks, and she'd given me some pointers. She'd gotten Zelda to sleep sometimes five hours a night, which everyone assured us was a lot, but for a woman used to logging a solid nine or ten hours of sleep a night, it wasn't much comfort.

I was epically unprepared, yes, but I was also very committed to putting in the required effort. I don't like to half-ass things; I'd waited a long time to have a baby. I wanted to do a good job. No, the best job. I wanted to be a superb mother.

But we didn't really know what to do a lot of the time.

"Now what?" we asked ourselves.

What a question.

We would spend the next months trying to answer that question every day anew. For now, we had no idea, and that seemed sort of okay. I started to feel better almost immediately after Zelda was born, and often that tided me over: at least I could go back to not worrying about my own body. Focusing on others has always been my wheelhouse. This was a job I could do. Anxiety, stress, crippling indecision? I could handle these from moment to moment. Sometimes, everything didn't *seem* okay, of course, like when I became gripped by the fear that my daughter was suffering from extreme jaundice. I should have known that, even if her very mild jaundice didn't improve on its own, there are easy and effective treatments. Instead, I spent the few spare moments I had to myself in the first week of her life furiously Googling "severe jaundice." I sometimes expected the worst when we took her for her doctor's appointments, which were every few days at first because she was born a little early.

It was only there in the warm, well-lit safety of the pediatrician's office that I felt at ease for the first month of Zelda's life. Once we got inside, I didn't want to leave. I wanted to stand over my daughter on the table, naked on a roll of white paper, and hear her doctor pronounce her beautiful and perfect over and over. Because when we got home, I sometimes secretly worried that something might be wrong: oh, she looked perfect to me, but I feared that she wasn't. I worried about the sound of her loud breathing. I worried that her nose, which was still smushed down from months of being pressed against the inside of my belly, was stuffed with something that shouldn't be there. I worried that she would die in her sleep even though I hovered over her. I knew my worries were the dumb fears of a novice. I knew that an overwhelming majority of the time, babies were just fine. I knew that she was fine, and yet the doubt and anxiety of the new mother was there, just under the surface. I'd worried through my pregnancy. I didn't want to worry through this part, too.

But I learned very early that sometimes my seemingly random fears were not entirely wrong: on one visit to the doctor when Zelda was only a few days old, I insisted that her stuffy nose was more than the nothing both the pediatrician and Josh assured me it was. Josh knew I was on edge. I couldn't blame him for thinking I was overreacting; I over-reacted to so much at first. But earlier in the morning, before we'd taken Zelda to the appointment, when I was dressing her on the changing table in her sunny bedroom, I'd caught a glimpse up her nose. Okay, I was looking for something, yes; but I thought I saw something up her left nostril. They were so tiny it was hard to tell. I asked the doctor to look with a flashlight. She did.

"I see nothing. Loud nose breathing is quite normal in infants. They don't know how to breathe out of their mouths yet," she assured me. I knew this, I'd Googled. It was the source of some pain to new mothers, as colds and stuffy noses mean obstructed breathing if one doesn't default to the mouth for air.

But I insisted: "There's something up there, I know it," I repeated. I could feel the room overflowing with something like sympathy for me. But the doctor looked again, and I crouched in with her.

"Look!" I said. "Do you see that?"

She nodded and got out tweezers, inserting them into Zelda's nostril. The baby started to fuss as she pulled out a large, dark green booger.

"This is meconium," she said, clearly impressed that I had seen it, stuffed so far up Zelda's nose.

I learned, then and there, that it was okay to default back to my "holy shit, something is wrong!" state, even if I was committed to trying to be a cool mom, a laid-back type. Nothing comes easily to me. Had my mother gone through moments of terrific anxiety when I was little?

I remember the times where I was sick, laying in a dark room with an earache or a sore throat or a flu, with a bowl to throw up in by the bed. My mother would swoop in silently throughout the night, touch my face, and adjust my blankets. Her hands were her thermometer. I don't remember her ever using a real one. She seemed to know everything, to be able to heal quietly. I know everyone probably thinks of their mom this way in early childhood, but what struck me as I started my own journey down the path of motherhood was how little of that I felt. My hands weren't thermometers, so I found myself constantly probing my young daughter's butt "just to check." Surely knowledge would come with time and experience, but at first I didn't feel any confidence. I didn't know what urges or fears to trust, which ones (most of them) were bogus phantoms creeping up on me to no good purpose.

And most of all, I worried that Zelda wasn't getting enough to eat.

There are lots of schools of thought on breast-feeding, and

I even have one of my own. It goes something like this: it's great, but also feeding a baby formula is fine, too. When my daughter was two weeks old and had lost weight at two consecutive doctor's appointments, we called in a lactation specialist. This was a person whose entire purpose, it seemed, was to help me on my quest to never feed my daughter formula. She wandered into our house with a giant medical scale, stripped Zelda down, and weighed her. Then, she had me nurse her while we sat there talking about how often I fed her. To her credit, this lactation specialist was the first person who suggested that a feeding schedule might help some of my woes. I was, up until then, simply jamming my breast into the baby's mouth as often as it seemed necessary, which was every hour or even less. The specialist suggested that if I put her on a better schedule, I would feel more comfortable knowing that she wasn't hungry and that Zelda would begin to make sense of her life a little. She'd know when to expect food, and that this could, the lactation specialist said, lead to a better sleeping schedule. All of this made sense to me. I asked about formula as she put Zelda on the scale. She'd gained 2 ounces from the feeding.

"You have enough milk," she declared, and this was indeed reassuring. "Feed her at the intervals I suggested, and I think she will have gained weight at her next appointment."

But she didn't. When that appointment rolled around several days later, she was exactly the same weight as she'd been the previous week. I asked the doctor about bottle-feeding her formula. My breasts were filled with milk that the baby simply didn't seem to be able to get out. I'd started pumping it, just to get it out. I was freezing it dutifully. The doctor agreed: "Feed the baby your bottle pumped milk or formula if you like after she has nursed. If she takes it, she's still hungry."

I worried that this would confuse my daughter about nipples: that bottle-feeding would make her reject my boob because the bottle was so much easier. That was, after all, what I read on the mommy blogs, an internet-based hell world I had lived for decades not even knowing it existed. But in those days, I was steeped in its worries and conspiracy theories. I worried that Zelda might reject the formula because it tasted as bad as it smelled. And I worried a little that I would be judged by other mothers if they saw me out and about bottle-feeding.

But I worried *more* that she wasn't eating enough. I remember quite clearly the first night that I bottle-fed her—not even formula, but breast milk I had pumped in an effort to help a painful clogged duct I had. "I feel like she's not eating enough and that's why she's unhappy!" I yelled into the phone to my husband, who was out desperately searching for some supply we needed. She was probably three weeks old. "Just give her the bottle. You'll see how much she drinks; you'll know she isn't hungry," he said. I took it over to her in her little basket, and she sucked down all three ounces in just a few minutes. I worried that I'd fed her too fast; that she would spit up. I worried that I'd sanitized the bottle wrong.

But she didn't spit up. She didn't reject my boob, or the bottle, or even the formula I guiltily started feeding her weeks later when my freezer stash ran out, when my boobs were sucked and pumped dry. She couldn't get enough to eat; she was hungry all the time. Every three hours like the consultant had said, I stuffed my breast into her mouth and she sucked whatever she could get for fifteen, thirty minutes.

Then she sucked down a bottle, first three, then four, then five ounces.

She began to gain weight rapidly, and the stress drained away from me. The doctor said, "Go for it," when I told her I thought she could use a faster-flowing nipple on the bottles because it took so long to feed her one. She didn't spit up. She didn't reject anything. Any white fluid in a bottle she'd drain down; the brand didn't matter. She would have taken milk straight from a cow or another woman's breast. She was getting fat. She went from being in the tenth percentile for weight to the eightieth in the space of two months.

I became, over the year or so that I read about breast-feeding issues and all the many politics surrounding our maternal bodies, something of a proselytizer for feeding babies however. "Whatever works!" I yelled to the women who told me that formula was not as good as breast milk. I decided that the most important thing for our family was that she ate enough, plain and simple. That she was not hungry, ever. This is the best advice I can give to other mothers.

But I struggle still with the guilt put on women who need to, or choose to, feed their babies formula. I'm not sure that, given the opportunity to have another child, I wouldn't go straight to a bottle of formula from the start. And though I know that this is a controversial position, it's one that I feel very proud of holding: for me, breast-feeding was fraught with emotional difficulty. After weeks of feeling as though I was simply starving my daughter, the ability to measure sometimes felt like a great gift. The ability to know, week in, week out, that this little girl, who had been born a little early and was a little small through no fault of her own, was now gaining weight, was very important to me.

Motherhood was challenging and tiring. I simply didn't want to also have to worry that she was starving, on top of everything else that we faced.

I didn't want to admit I needed help with getting my daughter to sleep either, but the baby nurse I'd hired had shown me, in a small space of time, that babies could be encouraged to sleep without simply letting them scream in their cribs. I didn't want to leave my baby alone in her bedroom with a stranger simply so that I could sleep, but I was so tired and sore that I relented. And I learned from her that sleep, for Zelda and for me, was possible.

And so sleep became my next obsession, after I'd figured out how to feed the baby in a way that made everyone happy and full. I'd never read a baby sleep book before I was pregnant (why would *anyone* do that?), but while I was pregnant, the subject of sleep training had come up with Josh's cousin, one of the only people in our families with small children. He mentioned using a book by Dr. Ferber with his two boys, so a few days later, I dutifully bought the new and revised edition of *Solve Your Child's Sleep Problems* by Richard Ferber. Next I tore through *The Happiest Baby on the Block*. But then, bored out of my mind and still only halfway through pregnancy, I gave up.

I was barely sleeping at night, even though Zelda had slept a bit better since the nurse. The nurse had given me, in fact, my first taste of confidence as a mother, the kind of stuff I assumed would have come directly from my own mother, had she been alive. Her little nuggets of wisdom—"Don't rush right over if you hear her stirring, you might wake her up"— were the first glimpse I had of something resembling a "schedule," or a light at the end of what seemed at that time to be an endless tunnel. But these tips—to let the baby settle herself, to not panic or rush, to be sure she had a full stomach before putting her to bed—didn't come from my mother. Maybe it was better that way; maybe I would have resisted my mother's help. As it was, I accepted the nurse's offered tips and took them to heart quickly.

No one had actually prepared me for the loss of time I experienced as a first-time, new mother. People told me I wouldn't sleep or shower, that I would worry over little nothings. All of it was true, and yet it wasn't the major thing I experienced. What knocked me out of sync with the rest of the world was that I suddenly felt as though I was no longer a part of it. I'd always been a loner, going days sometimes without talking to anyone besides my husband, and if he went away on business, I sometimes saw no one at all. I had only a few close friends from childhood, and none who I was in constant contact with, none who lived nearby.

And yet I was still unprepared for the level of isolation and time dissonance that I experienced when I was at home with Zelda for those first weeks and months.

Suddenly there was no difference between day and night: I was being led by a crazy worm who seemed unsatisfied even with food and cuddling—the only things I could offer her in abundance. I followed her blindly for weeks, stumbling around in various postpartum sweat suits that even I, a rather slovenly, careless dresser, would normally not wear outdoors. It was so bitterly cold that even hardy New Yorkers seemed to have hunkered down for just exactly the few weeks that we were also adjusting to our new reality. I looked out the window forlornly and the streets were empty, the trees had no leaves. It seemed the sun didn't come out from behind the clouds for days, which of course I knew would only make the baby's nonexistent jaundice worse. "Put the baby by a window!" a website I read, laughing hard enough to choke seltzer out of my nose, unhelpfully suggested. There was no fucking sun, and it seemed to be twenty degrees colder near the windows.

For the first time in years, I felt at sea even though I had lots to do: the laundry alone was constant. A newborn isn't exactly a lot of physical labor, but it's a constant drone of needing to be there, on, and paying attention. I could look at my phone a lot or read a bit of a book here and there, but I often found that I had no desire to. My daughter, such as she was, was very, very cute, but she had no personality to speak of that I could discern. I didn't hold that against her! But I felt, especially in the long winter days that made up that first month and a half, the weight of loneliness for the first time in my adult life. Rather than cherish the quiet of winter alone, I sensed myself on the verge of losing it. Mostly because I was tired, I know now.

The period where Zelda didn't sleep was short. It was laughably short if I compare myself to many other mothers, although I broke down very quickly. By the time Zelda was a month or so old, I ordered a new spate of baby sleep books. And though I don't remember who recommended the two that would come to form the core of my philosophy on baby sleep, I do remember, will always keep on the shelves of my library, those two books. They are worth hundreds, possibly thousands of dollars to me.

I need to stop here and explain why sleeping infants are such a big deal. And I also need to say, though I'm sure I've already explained: I fucking love to sleep. I don't know what my parents did with their house full of four children all pretty close in age, but we all sleep like logs. I remember my father tucking me in at night, and I remember waking up in the morning. I do not recall any up-all-nights, aside from that story about the puzzles and the occasional illness. We were, the four of us, robustly healthy, good sleepers. That said: I know nothing of their methods, and all the parents of the '70s and '80s I've asked about sleeping have been, it's no exaggeration to say, a little mysterious about their methods. "Oh, she was just a great sleeper," they'll say. Or, if you ask about babies crying in the middle of the night, they'll deny that ever happened. "Let them cry? No, never." I've come to believe, after the arduous work of teaching my own daughter to sleep, that parents lie, they forget, and those who raised children in the pre–baby monitor eras had an easier time of it.

At home with my newborn in our technologically advanced hell house, we could hear every errant gas passing and sigh. And of course, at first, besides those nights with the baby nurse, we'd sleep with Zelda in a bassinet beside our own bed, often waking her when we came to bed at 10:00 p.m. We realized this quickly, so at first we simply gave in and got into bed at 7:30 p.m. and lay there, plastered to the bed, trying not to move or make any noise, knowing all the while of course that she'd be awake in less than an hour anyway.

And that's why sleep is such a huge deal to parents: babies don't know how to do it. They don't have a clue. There's a period when they're first born, which lasts a week or so, which I refer to as "the lie," where they sleep happily and sort of soundly wherever you leave them—a couch, a box, whatever. But that ends hard and fast and soon, and you're screwed because you simply didn't know, if you're like we were. No one told me: babies don't know how to sleep. You need to help them.

And that was when I realized, through searching the internet, that, like breast-feeding, sleep training, closely associated with a technique called "cry it out" (you can, I believe, gather what it requires from its name), is a vast political war among parents of the current era. And it's fucked up.

There are two schools of thought on sleep training: those who say you can and should start it around two months of age up to about six months of age, and they are mostly backed up by research, modern medicine, and every pediatrician I've ever talked to. There are a million sleep-training techniques (hence all those books on Amazon.com), but most of them eventually involve a little "crying it out," where you simply let the baby cry in its crib in the hopes that it will fall to sleep on its own and forget to wake up. It sounds as though it won't work, but believe me, it does. I know dozens of parents who have done it, and our pediatrician, who runs a massive practice, swears by doing it at as early an age—eight weeks— as possible, simply because younger babies cry for fewer nights than older ones, who've been on the planet longer and know more, do.

The other camp, which has a large crossover in the Venn diagram with the breast-feeding-only camp, the organic-only camp, the no-sugar camp, the possibly anti-vaxx crowd, suggest that crying is bad for babies. There is very little evidence to back this up, but they say it anyway. They also say— I've heard them say it to me—that sleep training doesn't "work." That each baby is different, that you have to re–sleep train often, etc. I didn't know what to think, but my gut told me that simply "going with the flow" and "letting the baby guide me," as the no-sleep-train crowd suggested, was simply insane. No one was happy there in the house when we were all under-slept.

But I hoped to find a middle ground. I wanted to sleep train Zelda. I believed that sleep training her was for her own good. I could tell, even very early, that she was fussy, not because she was naturally hungry or miserable but because she was exhausted and didn't know how to stay asleep long enough to actually feel refreshed. But I didn't really relish the idea of letting her cry for a few nights in a row. She was, when I started my sleep-training research, too young as far as my pediatrician was concerned anyway: as I said, she recommended waiting until babies were eight weeks old and a certain weight in order to ensure they didn't actually need to eat in the middle of the night. But then I found a book that suggested I could start her sleep-training journey earlier—at birth, actually, if I'd discovered it then—with no crying involved.

The Baby Whisperer Solves All Your Problems is in my top five books I've ever read, alongside *Jane Eyre* and *The Blind Assassin*. It's the most important book I have ever owned. Because it worked. I read this book cover to cover when Zelda was about five weeks old and immediately decided to try out the author's system, even though it was intense. Actually, the fact that the Baby Whisperer, whose real name was Tracy Hogg, had so many goddamned rules was probably what drew me to her insanity. A small sampling of her technique includes the fact that the infant should almost always sleep in its bed—not a stroller or a rocker—overnight as well as for naps. This means, essentially, that while the process of sleep training is going on, you're chained to the house. She isn't totally specific on how long each baby will take to "sleep through the night," but says they usually get to that by three months of age. Literally can't leave almost ever, because infants sleep so often. She also suggested that the baby sleep in its own room, outfitted with blackout shades and a white-noise machine. She insisted that there be a bedtime routine that was exactly the same every single night. That the baby went to sleep at very specific intervals after being awake for very specific periods of time. Feeding must happen when the baby wakes up, not when it's going to sleep, which is a secret weapon of most new mothers: feed the little shit to sleep. No, no, said Tracy. That would be an "unhealthy" sleep association. I hated Tracy, but I felt compelled to test her.

At first, her schedule (which she insists is *not* a schedule, but it totally is) seemed insane. One day, a week or so into it, Josh said, "This is crazy, this is miserable, what are we even doing this for?" but I persisted. "Give me until eight weeks," I said. If, when we got to eight weeks and we took her to the pediatrician and she was still sleeping badly, waking up every three hours, I'd admit failure and we'd do the fast-and-easy cry it out.

I trusted Tracy, as I trusted the baby nurse before her, because I investigated enough to know that on a basic level what she was saying made a lot of sense. But because Tracy was not accessible to me in any way, I couldn't get her feedback: I was on my own, floundering around, rereading the same passages questioning myself. I needed her authority, I needed her confidence, and because I didn't have a mother of my own, Tracy became almost a real person in my mind. She was distant, she seemed to know everything, and, in the end, I had nobody but myself to blame if it didn't work.

It didn't seem to be working for those first few days, as I dutifully noted each time she ate, how much she ate, when she went down, when she woke up. Every day of that time period is etched on me like a tattoo. It was miserable at first. I'd do what Tracy said, get Zelda into her crib "awake but drowsy" for a nap, leave the room, and she'd wake up twenty-four minutes later. I wanted to scream a lot for those few days. I'd drag myself up the stairs, my body feeling heavy, my mind full of the doubt that I dared not admit even to Josh. Jesus, this couldn't possibly work.

But about a week after we started, she got a little better. And by the time she was eight weeks old, she was down to waking just once a night, around 2:00 in the morning. The pediatrician told us we could let her cry at night now if we wanted. I said I thought she might actually sleep through the night on her own; she was just waking up once at night to eat, and she seemed very hungry then. The doctor gave me good advice: "Why don't you try letting her cry at the beginning of sleep if needed, to go down, but not in the middle of the night if you're not ready yet?" I decided to try that. Zelda cried one or two nights at bedtime, for fifteen minutes each. She'd already gotten used to our routine, and part of Tracy's entire scheme was in fact to ensure that when you tried to put your baby to bed, she was actually tired anyway, so she would fall to sleep easily. Zelda by then had been on this routine for a few weeks, and she was indeed very tired at naps and bedtime. After that, there was almost never any bedtime crying.

By ten weeks, my daughter began sleeping "through the night" as they say, on her own, without ever "crying it out": from about 7:00 p.m. to 7:00 a.m. I could tell you how that came to be, but it would be a book in itself. I took notes and obsessed for a month. I worried about nothing else. We barely left the house to get the napping schedule just right. But at the end of it, I was gifted a great sleeper, a baby who rarely—maybe ten times in her entire life—wakes up after we put her to bed. We were gifted an even happier kid, who was so rarely cranky or crying. We were gifted our nights to do with as we wished. At first I mostly slept, of course. I went to bed sometimes moments after she closed her eyes.

The change in her was unmistakable, remarkable: she was a different baby after she passed the ten-week mark. And the change in me was pretty obvious too, once a few weeks of she's-going-to-wake-up panic passed. I still sleep with a baby monitor nearby, and Zelda is three and a half. I still worry that she will wake in the middle of the night, but I can count on my fingers the number of times that has happened. She sleeps well when we travel, when we accidentally miss bedtime by a few minutes, when she's in the car. She even slept well, the nurses marveled over how well, in a pediatric unit for a three-day pneumonia hospital stay when she was two years old. "Nobody sleeps eleven hours a night here!" the nurse cried, and I could see why, with them coming in every hour to check on her or give her oxygen, bells ringing and equipment humming. But my Zelda: she's the best.

And I have the luxury of smiling when people tell me I "got lucky" with a good sleeper. Sure, I did; I know it. But I also put in a stiff five weeks of effort on her behalf, and I almost never deviate from her bedtime routine even now. It's not negotiable. It's my thing. And we all have benefited from it immensely.

I'm probably (I assume this is now obvious) prouder of getting Zelda to sleep well than anything else I've achieved as a parent. Did my own parents work this hard to get their kids to sleep? I have no idea. It's lost to time. There are many ways to skin the cat; we both got there somehow.

When my brother John was still a baby, we shared a bedroom before we moved to McMurray. I remember once waking up early in the morning, and he was still asleep. I wandered over to look at him in his crib and woke him up. Not wanting to expose myself as a baby waker, I went downstairs to my mother, who was on the phone, and said, "The baby is awake." She hung up her call and took me to the foot of the stairs, where you could sit and hear what was going on in the kids' bedrooms upstairs. I used to occasionally catch her there, at the bottom of the stairs, just listening to what the four of us were doing up there. She leaned over and said to me, "Shhhh, listen." I listened and could hear John upstairs in his crib babbling to himself. She took me back to the kitchen and got out the cereal for my breakfast.

"He's fine up there," she said. "Even babies need private time. If he's not crying, it's okay to let him there for a little while."

I don't have a huge store of these moments in my memory, just a few. But as I became a mother, actively learning how to parent, they bubbled up to the surface. How I remembered them changed or what they meant changed to me. It seemed my mother had given me just a little advice a really long time ago.

I'd always assumed this was some kind of laziness on my mother's part, though lazy was not part of her character in any way. She was overworked with her kids, and so I didn't judge, but even at five or six, I sort of thought, "Well, she doesn't feel like getting him yet."

But after Zelda was born and after she was sleep trained,

I made a rule: I didn't get up until 7:00 and get her out of bed, even if she was awake. I just let her loll around in there, and at first she cried sometimes. But then, very quickly, she stopped. Mostly she slept until 7:00, but there were occasional mornings when she simply woke up early and babbled to herself. Even for naps I made a policy of not immediately rushing in to her at the first signs of waking, because I realized, thirty years later, that my mother was right: the baby wasn't just fine in there, she was actually doing something important. She was waking up. She was adjusting to being awake. And eventually, I started to notice that she seemed to be working on learning how to talk there, in her crib, all alone. "Ba ba ba ba ba," you'd hear over and over, her feet in her hands.

"The baby's awake!" anyone who was in the house would inevitably tell me anytime they heard her stirring, maybe expecting me to flutter up the stairs as fast as I could. But I didn't, I don't. The few times I did rush in to her, she cried and seemed generally unhappy to see me. It's changed in the past few years, of course, and now that she can speak, well, her desires are not a mystery: "Mommy, I'm awake!" I hear some mornings. Sometimes I just get the opening strains of a song. But I know now for sure that my mother was right: babies need private time. And nothing made me prouder than the first day Zelda closed the door to her room, saying to me, "I just need some privacy." ("I dusht need some primacy.") Amen.

CHAPTER 6

* * *

There was a long period of my childhood—say, from the time I was in third grade up through middle school—where, if I didn't have Emily sleeping over, my mother got in bed with me at my bedtime and we lay together, each reading our own books. I can still see her there now, bathed in warm lamplight, laying on her stomach, propped up on her arms, staring down at a book.

I had a large double bed in my room, an antique bed that was hulking and a little weird compared to all my friends' beds—regular modern twins—that my mother and my grandma Elly had bought together at a vintage store.

I never really questioned why my mother slept with me, and though I know now it was evidence of problems in my parents' marriage, I accepted her explanation: my father worked very early, he went to bed earlier than she did, and he didn't like the lights on when he was sleeping. My father is not a reader. I can sympathize with this arrangement, having been married for a decade: it's very annoying if your schedules are at all out of sync and if one of you is a reader but the other is not. This is an underexplored topic of marriage, I feel. If you're a reader paired off with a not-reader or, worse, an in-bed TV watcher paired off with a not-in-bed TV watcher, well, someone will have to give.

My mother was a reader. We spent quiet time together in bed reading side by side, not talking. This was something I knew I'd like to have with Zelda. An almost passive but meaningful part of my relationship with my mother was our love of books.

Some of the first things I bought for Zelda when I was pregnant, as I said, were books. It would be hard to overstate my attachment to my own books, as physical objects I must lug around and move with me and as emotional necessities. Whenever we travel, I often take a dozen books with me instead of the proper clothing, simply because I'm never sure what I'll be in the mood for.

This is, I know, not a unique or outstanding feature. But I think it is the most important one about me.

And then the first meaningful interactions between Zelda and me were the long, sunny days spent in her bedroom where she, just fed and awake from a nap, would lay on her back in her crib and listen to me read. I didn't feel completely natural carrying on a one-sided conversation with her, even though she was a few months old by then and we spent all our mornings together alone. We ventured out to meet Kim and Amy or other friends in the afternoons, but mornings were just ours, and I filled them, determined not to baby talk to her too much, by reading.

It was partly selfish, of course: I missed reading books, but at night after she went to bed I often found that I was too tired to read and ended up falling asleep in front of the television or just getting straight into bed at 8:00 or 9:00 p.m. Babies are so much more exhausting than people tell you, even the ones who, like Zelda, are "easy."

And she was. "Oh, you have an easy baby," everyone always told me. I could never quite tell if that was a compliment or an accusation, if it was said with admiration or with something else, something akin to jealousy but also the kind of competitiveness that happens to new parents, where having challenges stack up is a mark of how well you're doing. Some claim that easy babies are easy through no doing of yours, but that's not true, of course. I take some credit for Zelda's good moods, mostly because I taught her to sleep as well as I myself sleep. But her good nature, her sunny disposition, I don't take credit for that.

The hours we spent in the first year of her life there, in her room, in the mornings, are times I will never, ever forget. She humored me as I read. I started with little picture books with few words but realized very quickly that a book that took two minutes to read wasn't enough.

When I was pregnant, I had bought several books for her that I'd remembered fondly as a child. There sat on her shelf next to the white-noise machine and the board books, the stuffed animals and chew toys, ten or so chapter books I loved in fourth grade.

At random, and partly because it had some pictures I could show her, I chose to read *Little House in the Big Woods* to Zelda first. It took about a week to complete.

Reading aloud is an odd experience, especially when your audience is one person incapable of feedback. I read until she fussed and then gave up. At first she could listen only for two or three minutes without squirming around and making noise, trying to see where I was as I sat in a chair by the window or paced the short distance of her tiny bedroom. But soon she began to be quiet for much longer periods, and I found that she was listening to me.

I read *Alice's Adventures in Wonderland* and *Island of the Blue Dolphins*, another problematic classic. I cried my way through *The Little Prince* and slogged through *The Wizard of Oz*, a book that I'd only thought I had read as a child, it turned out. Dorothy wasn't my kind of girl, always whining to go home. I'll admit my empathy level was possibly at an all-time low for anyone outside of that little room. "Oh, she's crying for home again," I thought to myself. But Zelda would eventually love the story and now often takes the book to bed with her. "I love *The Wizard of Woz*," she says. "But not the bad witch."

I read to her for hours, partly because I wanted to get rid of so many hours and partly because, I see now, I didn't have much to say to her yet. Only in the space since my daughter has turned three years old have I ever begun to "miss the baby months," as they say. And only a little bit at that. The baby phase was very hard for me. I bonded to her, I loved her, and she was very easy, always smiley, almost never crying, but still, I struggled through those months.

I thought of my mom in those hours I sat in Zelda's bedroom, on the rug or in the armchair three feet from her crib, reading to her. My mother hadn't struggled like this, or if she had, she hadn't ever bothered to tell anyone. To hear her story, she was as happy as she'd ever been when there was a baby in the house. Only when we moved, when we were all finally in school and she had some of the peace and quiet I now often mourned the lack of, did she seem to falter.

I wasn't yet sure what I was supposed to be doing. Zelda required constant attention when awake, as far as I could tell, but, beyond that, nothing taxed my brain. It felt like a marathon of boringness. I sometimes wondered at the veracity of my mother's account of life with children. Though Zelda was fascinating and I could stare at her toes with amazement, there are so many hours in one single day. I'd never simply spent so much time with another person, not doing anything at all, no conversation, no real interactions. Just her and me, staring at each other, singing little songs, talking nonsense, reading books.

I see now that reading wasn't the worst solution. I'm not sure whether Zelda got anything out of it. I told myself that I was helping her to learn patience and to listen, but really, I was just getting by. I didn't feel unhappy; in fact, I think of those days very fondly, so lazy and full of nothing. But for the first time in my life that I could remember, I lacked a clear purpose. I had no vocation that I could see. Oh, I had to keep the baby alive, and she was stimulating in ways I'd never encountered before, but we were separate people, and her prerogatives overwhelmed my own. I read to her because I wanted to be reading, because I needed mental exercise, and this was the only time I could find for it.

It was the first time in my adult life where *just living* was the rule of the day. I'd left home at eighteen and worked and gone to school every day since then. I'd taken only two or three vacations in that time. I woke up mostly early and went to bed after midnight, filling the space between with work and reading and cooking. I've never been good at sitting and watching a movie—Josh has never gotten used to my multitasking habit of reading while watching TV—or just hanging around. When I wake up I immediately get dressed, brush my teeth, and head to the kitchen to begin my day.

Now that Zelda is a toddler, her pace and mine are aligned. We wake and begin, there are tasks, lunches to make, breakfasts to have, errands to run, and school to go to. But when faced with this first part of her life, before I'd figured out that we could venture into the wilderness together, we simply were.

I started taking her to the restaurant down the street from our house as soon as it got warm enough for us to walk the three blocks there. Sometimes we met Kim and Amy or another friend, but often we were alone. Weekend brunches were often stressful: Josh was home, and getting three people out the door is infinitely more complicated than getting two out. And of course in Brooklyn, Saturday or Sunday brunch was always crowded. But Zelda and I, we could manage on a weekday, sometimes barely, occasionally beautifully. Out and about was where I began to see how she and I would be together, to spy what our dynamic might be in the future.

At the end of that street we'd sit, at first inside because it was too cold, eventually at a little table outside once it was warm and sunny, and just look at each other. She'd sit in her giant stroller and, eventually, in a little wooden restaurant high chair. At first she'd have a bottle while I had coffee or wine, and later she'd eat her vegetable baby food pouches. I stared at her; she stared at me.

One afternoon we'd been out for a while at the park with Kim and Amy, who had headed home for dinner. It was fall; Zelda was probably seven months old. It had been a long day, as all days were then. I was tired, but bedtime, which was at 7:00 p.m., seemed so far away at that moment. Josh wasn't going to be home before bedtime; it was only us. And as we passed the restaurant on our way home, on a whim, I stopped, parked the stroller, and sat down at a table.

A waiter came over and handed me a menu. Zelda looked up at me, smiling from her stroller, as I unlocked it and moved the seat upward so that she was "sitting." I looked through my bag. I didn't have any milk for her or even a bottle of water. I let her sip from my glass, which she always loved. Zelda was a self-feeder from day one, grabbing the spoon from my hand the first time I fed her solids. She let me hold her bottles for her for months longer than most babies, but she always grabbed for forks and adult glasses.

This water was seltzer, and she sputtered it out a little, then reached for more. I had a pouch of apricots, which she never really liked but which would do. I ordered a watermelon salad, hoping she would be open to sharing it with me. I looked around at the beautiful, waning day, the sun just going down over the East River, visible in the not very distant distance. One other person, a nicely dressed woman, was on the sidewalk sitting at a table, drinking wine. I ordered a glass of wine and drank my first sip too avidly, feeling the wine dribble down the front of my shirt. I looked down as I started to sponge it up with a napkin and noticed that my shirt was covered in other stains, not just the wine. There was old milk, maybe some tomato sauce. Was I still wearing my clothes from the day before?

I shuddered to think of my hair, which I'd stopped cutting and styling and which I washed only a few times a week. I looked like shit, I was sure of it. And for me, this is saying a lot, because even on my best days I look only moderately put together. I've never been a "good dresser." Anyway, the woman sitting there alone at the table who shamed me simply by existing was reading *The New Yorker*. I had a stack of *New Yorker*s at home, by my side of the bed. I often pondered not reading them but simply tying them together with some heavy twine and throwing them onto the curb. When would I be able to read *The New Yorker* again? When would I want to? I still went to bed exhausted at 9:30 or 10:00 p.m. and was barely making time to start writing again. I was still drained and had little interest in showering. I didn't feel unhappy, but I felt like a completely different person than the one who had decided, finally, to have a baby.

I thought the woman sitting there alone, with the good haircut and the glass of wine, must be judging me somehow. She must feel very smug about her decision not to have kids or to remain happily single. I didn't know anything about her other than that, and though I didn't exactly envy her, I felt very certain she did not envy me. She caught me staring at her; we made eye contact. I looked away in what felt like shame and put my sunglasses on.

Down the street I could hear the familiar sounds of kids screaming, playing, wringing the last fun out of the end of the day. And in the distance, a crying baby.

As I looked down at Zelda, who had been fussing because she wanted ever-increasing volumes of seltzer, which I didn't want to give her because there was no place to change her closer than home, a calm washed over her. She smiled. She looked around, not needing me, me not needing her. She gave me another moment to contemplate the disgusting figure we cut, as I noted her little striped sundress was covered in red stains, too.

"Strawberries!" I almost said aloud. We'd both eaten

them for breakfast. That must have been what was on both of our fronts. Strawberries. We love strawberries.

The crying baby was getting closer, and in fact I could see it now, or its vehicle: a stroller identical to Zelda's, an Uppababy Cruz, rolling toward us down the sidewalk. A man was pushing the stroller calmly and silently, as if the baby inside was not wailing its head off, as if it was the most normal thing in the world. "Must be a newborn," I said to myself, looking down at my half-year-old baby with appreciation. One thing we had conquered: Zelda never screamed in her stroller anymore. I guess those days were over.

I'd been there, where he was, not very long ago, just trying to hold it together when every moment outside of home seemed like a potential or certain disaster. I'd held back tears as strangers said, "Maybe she's hungry!" as I pushed a screaming baby down our street, pretending I didn't care that she was making the most amount of noise that she was capable of.

My deflated feelings of inadequacy passed; I felt slightly puffed up and more confident in the moment. That's how it works sometimes. The man with the stroller stopped at the table with the woman reading *The New Yorker*, the woman I now recognized as the mother of the screaming baby.

"I guess he's not going to sleep," she said to the man as he engaged the foot brake. "We should go then," she said, glancing at me and my now-silent baby.

"How old is he?" I asked, sipping my glass of wine.

"Nine weeks tomorrow," she said, smiling weakly.

"How old is she?" She gestured to Zelda, who waved, smiling a drooly smile.

"Just passed seven months." I smiled back. Little old nine-weeks was still wailing, Dad desperately attempting to jam a pacifier into his mouth over and over. "Does it get easier?" he asked, looking up at me for the first time.

"Oh, we have our days," I said.

"This seems like one of the good ones," Mom said, jamming her *New Yorker* into the stroller.

"I guess so," I said, shrugging and smiling at my baby.

They went home, and then we went home. I washed the apricots from Zelda's face and put her in clean pajamas. I read to her and put her to bed, then showered off the dirt from my own body, standing in the hot water, not thinking about anything at all.

The next morning, I pulled a new book from the shelves. "Do you want to read *The Secret Garden*?" I asked, fumbling around. "Or . . . *The Canterbury Tales*?" Zelda was laying in her crib in a sundress, already dressed for the day. I'd laid it out the night before, knowing it was going to be very hot. The sun was already beating inside her room; the air conditioner was quietly blowing.

"Actually," I said, looking at my watch. It was 8:00 in the morning. Josh wasn't awake yet. "Let's go out. The coffee shops are open at least," I said. We went out. But eventually, we did read both *The Secret Garden* and *The Canterbury Tales*. She preferred the latter, I think.

I never liked other people's babies before I had one myself. It hadn't occurred to me that sometimes you need to fly home for your grandmother's funeral, and the baby still exists. The baby has to fly with you. I had spent much of my adult life being annoyed at them on airplanes and in public, never thinking about how important it actually was, and is, to take your babies out into the world as fast as possible, to make them unafraid and social, to teach them how to behave in a restaurant or a bookstore.

In the first half year of Zelda's life, I decided to do just that: to take her with me, within reason, wherever I myself needed or wanted to go. I sought out cafés and stores when they were least likely to be busy, off hours and away from huge crowds, where we could give it a shot, where we could test her patience and give her new experiences. She wasn't always in agreement; sometimes she cried. Once, we had to leave when the food took too long and she simply wasn't up to waiting. But over those months she learned very fast how to fit into the world, and, rather than making Earth conform to her, Zelda, always a fast learner, always pliable and happy to wave to strangers, conformed to whatever was around her.

I learned to live and breathe sometimes without a personal sense of purpose other than simply being alive. It was scary to not have something mentally exhausting to focus on, to have to be present rather than distracted and lost inside of myself all the time. But I thought I was managing most days to turn what felt like boredom into a virtue of sorts. I wasn't miserable or depressed. I was just different than I had been before.

And I learned to be more sympathetic to the screaming children around me. And the struggling parents. And of course I learned quickly to accept the people around me, often young but also often elderly, who simply didn't like my baby or want to indulge her with a wave or a smile. We all learn a lot, not just from books but from engaging with the world around us. Zelda reminded me of that.

◆　◆　◆

The defining characteristic of the first ten or fifteen years of my life was that I was an unapologetic bookworm. I probably spent more time alone in my bedroom reading or hiding from kids on the playground with a book than I did doing anything else. I learned to walk while holding a book, up the street to Emily's house or home from school. Occasionally, a car in my neighborhood would pull over so whatever adult was behind the wheel could tell me how dangerous what I was doing was. "You'll get hit by a car," the old lady who was so old she definitely shouldn't have been driving, who lived five houses up from ours, cackled at me. I remember thinking she sounded as though she wanted to help make it happen. Reading was probably some form of escape from my reality, but that thought never occurred to me back then.

I got this love of books from my mother, who ate every book she ever picked up like it was actual food, and from my second-grade teacher, Miss Zimmerman. My mother never censored what I read; her library, full of classics and true crime and Stephen King, was sitting there, in the piles she kept by her bed and on the shelves in the basement, available to me whenever I wanted. I asked for books for Christmas and birthdays, and one Christmas, my grandfather built shelves to hang on the wall of my bedroom so that I could begin to amass my own tiny collection.

◆　◆　◆

It was in middle school that we met Vanessa and Ellen. Emily and I had plenty of other girls in our circle of friends, but never had we really brought others into the fold of our own weirdness before. Vanessa and Ellen were different.

If I am remembering correctly, I brought Vanessa, and

Emily brought Ellen. Vanessa and Ellen, though, already knew each other. That was the deal going forward: Emily and I were a unit, and Vanessa and Ellen were one. Together, we were a dangerous Voltron of adolescent girlhood.

Sometimes, one of us (Emily or me) met another girl in school. We'd hang out with that new girl alone, perhaps at her house or our own and, if all went well, eventually we'd debut her to the other. No one really stuck until Vanessa and Ellen.

Vanessa was small and had long, flowing blond hair. She had already developed breasts, which was something none of the rest of us had done yet. Her family was from the Midwest somewhere, but she'd lived in McMurray most of her life. Ellen was exotically beautiful and nearly six feet tall. Vanessa and Ellen had gone to a different elementary school than Emily and me, and the four of us were dumped together starting in the sixth grade into the same middle school.

After that, from then until we graduated from high school, the four of us were a group package. And it was by way of there being a block of us, rather than just a pair, that we began to flourish into a really original group of human beings. Before, individually all of us had stuck out from the general crowds of kids. We weren't exactly popular, but we weren't really made fun of, either. I didn't quite fit into any group of children, and though I was growing somewhat comfortable with that, even misfits need their cliques. So we built one.

Emily was always in some ways the most solid of us: she made friends with more popular people easily, whereas I was clearly a loner who was happy to recede into the background. She did the best in school and worried endlessly about her grades. By middle school, I already didn't care. Although each of us had our own familial struggles that we talked about them in pairs, whispering around one another to avoid being confrontational, we mostly kept our secrets safe within ourselves. For all our daring, we couldn't quite divulge the things that our families did to fuck us up as a group. Not yet.

When my brother Daniel was starting kindergarten, I took him on the bus the first day. He sat next to me on the front seat, him with his little red He-Man backpack strapped on his back. And without a word of complaint, he threw up all over himself, vomit dripping onto the floor of the bus. I was paralyzed; I didn't know what to do. And more than anything, I felt anxious that other people would notice. The anxiety overwhelmed my worry about his well-being or my desire to help him. "How do I clean this up?" I wondered. The bus driver gave me a huge roll of those scratchy brown industrial paper towels, and we did the best we could. I remember Daniel crying a little bit and me trying to comfort him. "It's okay," I said. And he answered back, "It always is."

Years later, in high school, when I was in eleventh grade and Daniel in ninth, I walked down the hall to see him randomly being made fun of by some bigger, older bully. I don't remember what he said to Daniel, only that when I went over to him, Daniel said, "He sucks. I don't care if he thinks I'm cool or not." I've carried that comment with me ever since, because it rang true: Daniel, for whatever reason, decided very early in life never, ever to care what people thought of him, and it made him smarter than the rest of us, who worried over all the minor things that unpopular kids often worry over. The rest of my high school career, after that day when my younger brother taught me a way forward with a few tossed-off words, was more carefree than the previous decade had been.

But in middle school, I hadn't learned that yet. I still cared, even if only a little, what people thought of me. It was clear that I wasn't going to be a star student: I was flunking math classes every chance I got. I was bad at sports; I was bad at trying too hard, something that would stick with me, an unwillingness to try new things, not for fear of failure but simply because I had found the things I liked doing and wanted to do them. I was already, and would continue to be through even college and graduate school, the kind of person who cut classes to hide in the library reading.

But in this space of time, these middle school years, my parents began to recede into the background for me. They were in so many ways still all important: they had to buy me everything that I needed, and they needed to drive me from place to place if they weren't walking distance. And yet, they became almost background characters to the tumultuous requirements of my growing social life.

In some ways, my mother ceased to exist for me in middle school. I wasn't really interested in boys and didn't need her advice on the Big Topics. I hadn't gotten my period yet; I didn't need to wear a bra. My entire social life basically revolved around school and after-school activities like dances, plays, and occasionally hanging out at the public library in the afternoon, secretly cutting photos of Madonna from *Rolling Stone* magazine.

Emily, Vanessa, Ellen, and I carved out a space for ourselves. We passed notes, which were often thousand-word-long letters, among ourselves in classes. We made fun of other students and teachers relentlessly. We were all in band together, and we tried out for dance competitions together. We went to school dances and drank tiny bits of alcohol or smoked stray cigarettes together, huddled in school bathroom stalls. We built a new family for ourselves, and it subbed in for the ones we were born into. In many ways, we were still privately unhappy; this is true of all kids approaching their teenage years. Parents and family still controlled almost every move we made. I didn't have my own money; I couldn't drive. My parents held all the power, and though I didn't yet see them as enemies, I was starting to see them as foils at least. In this space, I think, my mother's drinking problem became progressively worse, but if anybody noticed, they didn't say much about it.

My mother was, I think I've strained to say, a very good mother. Sure, sometimes she didn't show up. But she usually did. And because she continued to be a devoted mother in those years, I think her problem was simply glossed over by everyone around her.

I kept my home life and my social life separate. My friends didn't come over to my house very much. That space was reserved for Emily, who I could keep in my room if my mother was acting erratic, but that mostly happened late at night anyway, when we were safely asleep. But I'm sure by then Emily knew exactly what was going on. My father seemed to be away for most of that time. I know that he wasn't, but in my memory, he had receded a bit, probably the way fathers do for many adolescent girls.

At home, I read and hung out with my brothers; I visited my grandparents and went to church on Sundays. In this space reserved for family, my mother taught me to bake pies from scratch and how to properly fold towels. How to iron a shirt and how to sew. We kept reading together.

All alcoholics live lives that are divided into at least two

lives: one where they are drinking, and one in which they are not. My life was divided too, and though the question of which life was the truer one for my mother troubled me greatly, the question of my own division seemed harmless to me. My own friends were experiencing, similar things to more or less the same degree: one life at home with family, one away with friends.

My mother kept drinking, was drinking more, in fact, but the drinking troubled me less somehow as I began to have my own personal life. I worried about her still, thought about her drinking constantly, but suddenly I had new ways of diverting my attention.

A kid that age shouldn't have to feel bad for her mother, but there were nights when I'd pretend to be asleep and just lay there rather than read in bed next to her. Something about her made me sad. I couldn't put my finger on what it was. I didn't fully rest it on the drinking, either. But soon, as I grew into a teenager, fighting with my mother over everyday things would become my primary way of interacting with her.

CHAPTER 7

• • •

It's incredibly weird to write a book about your child and not write about your marriage, when you're definitely married. Zelda definitely has a dad, his name is Josh, and he's my husband. He is absolutely not thirty-three Chihuahuas stacked in a trench coat. I assure you he is 100 percent real.

But I committed quite early, in the days of writing essays for public consumption about my life with my daughter, to not really saying anything about my marriage, simply because Josh, as a somewhat public person in his life as an editor and writer himself, never "signed up" for my project. He could have chosen to write about his experiences of fatherhood, but he didn't. I'm sure his version would be much different than mine.

And there was something too dear and near to me in the thought of writing honestly about my relationship with him.

But also: I don't remember that much of him in that first year. I have to try really hard to pull up memories of him sometimes, as if there was a finite amount of space inside then for storing things.

I know this is more my failing than his absence

motherhood-induced myopia, where all I could or would see was myself and my daughter and the various threads that tied us back and forth to each other. It was selfishness personified, a biological reaction. Taking care of a child is so hard, so time consuming: it made sense that our emotions and needs would consume me and that in turn, three years later, I would have a blank space for a lot of where Josh should be.

But also: I *did* spend much of my time with Zelda alone. The weekends were family time, and they were necessarily less stressful, simply because there were two sets of hands, two people to manage the packing up and the setting off. We were happy some days and miserable others. But most of the time he wasn't physically around. He was just getting mean, panicked, desperate, or even angry texts from me. It's not that he didn't suffer the emotional drain that comes with first-time parenthood, but he did experience a lot of it only secondhand.

And even though I did decide to leave him out of my writing largely, I feel I need to say something. I owe it to myself to be honest about how awful that first part of it really was.

Everyone who has ever had a child will say things like, "The first year is the worst," or, "Good-bye to having sex," really encouraging remarks that make you feel at once superior to them but also very sad for everyone. Sad, because it's almost always, from other mothers I've talked to, true: that blank memory space for me is partly blank because I expected the relationship I had with Josh to be on hold while I kept the baby alive. I struggled, sometimes alone but often with him by my side, to keep the fucking baby alive. To seem happy around her even if I felt as though I were drowning in the monotony or from exhaustion or the repetition of each identical day. I struggled to teach her to sleep and to make sure she was clean and healthy and happy.

But I soon realized we were succeeding. Our baby was magical and fun and cute and happy. She flourished as we treaded water beside her, hoping that once the struggles passed we would still *have* a relationship with each other. That our love would tide us over in the dark times.

Which isn't to say we didn't have sex or intimacy or that we didn't spend evenings together watching TV and eating bad takeout food. We did those things. But there were necessary changes, and it wasn't hours we lost. We'd both always worked a lot, and Josh had always traveled on business several weeks a year, so we were used to spending a lot of time apart and on our own. It was, mostly on my end, an emotional loss of space for him. I stopped worrying about him in the same way; I stopped caring so much and empathizing with him.

I don't believe the amount of caring we can produce is finite. But I do know, from the experience of having a child, that the first year of my daughter's life meant that there was for a while a finite number of places I could spend my love and empathy. I simply had to focus on keeping us alive. And "us" usually meant the two of us. I had to hope that everyone else could wait for a while.

I don't know why it was this way, only that it was and that I'm not alone, that other women have described similar paths in that first year or so.

I don't know if I can regret that it was this way because I'm not sure we could have managed any *other* way. I remember an argument we had late one night, when Zelda was asleep. We were arguing because Josh had come home very late. So late that I was struggling to stay awake and was ready for bed by the time he walked through the door. I stayed awake because I wanted to see him and because I knew he hated to come home to a house where everyone was sleeping; but I was angry to have to do it, because I was so tired. It was a very typical argument of the period.

"You don't know what it's like here, all day alone with her. I'm exhausted," I'd say, trying to work out why I was mad at him and at least partly resentful that he got to physically leave the premises for hours every day. But I was also tired and ready for bed and trying to stay up. I resented a lot those days, and though I didn't say it, I'm sure he felt it just the same.

"You don't know what it's like for me," he'd say. "I have to leave the house, be presentable, very early, and I don't get to see you or Zelda all day, and then I come home and everyone is asleep, and I do that for five days a week."

Both of us were right. For us, being parents at first meant constant competition about the very different levels of the other's burden and the incapacity for the other to understand that. It is, in hindsight, almost funny.

But that particular night the argument escalated and reached, unlike many previous arguments in the genre that had resulted in annoyance and stalemate, a revelation, at least for me.

"You can accept this or not: this is reality for now," he said, I thought a little harshly. I was prepared to bite back, thinking of how to respond, but he went on: "You will always have spent more time with her than me when this part of our lives is over. Nobody can change that. You can resent me for it, but you should also know that I will always be jealous, even if it's nice for me to get to leave. I can't get this time back, and neither can you." I wasn't sure whether he was actually jealous of me, but I took that night as a win.

It's not good to feel better about yourself because your partner expresses pain. But sometimes you have to accept realities. Sometimes you make the best of what you have on offer. I wouldn't change it, I guess.

Josh taught me the value of a good old-fashioned, out-loud fight. He taught me that early in our relationship; it was one of the things I liked about him. I came from a family where many things, from the small and relatively unimportant to the giant and possibly tragic, were often not engaged with openly. We didn't have huge fights in our family growing up. We kept our thoughts mostly to ourselves. There wasn't dishonesty: my parents taught me that lying was wrong, and I am still a terrible liar in the very few times I've attempted it. But there is a way to be dishonest without lying actively: choosing to say nothing is about the same as an open lie a lot of the time.

Josh came from a family where nothing was off-limits and everything was open to discussion. I was taken aback by their propensity for yelling openly at one another, even in front of interlopers like myself. Back in the earliest days of our relationship, when I was barely a known entity to Josh's brother and parents, I felt uncomfortable but energized by their ability to make decisions quickly, where my family, especially once my mother was dead, sometimes took hours to decide what to have for dinner simply because everyone failed to speak their mind in a timely fashion.

Every family operates differently. "You're all like your father!" my mother used to say in exasperation, years after my parents divorced. What she meant was that my brothers and me are sometimes stubbornly silent. And we are. I still feel that well inside of me when I am asked even simple, direct questions: a deep desire to simply say nothing, to refuse. To stay inside of myself. I am deeply solitary in a way that my mother never was.

My mother was, while my parents were still married and we were all living at home together, the decider. She was the one who moved us up and out of the house, who kept the gears oiled and the machinery working. "Time to go!" she'd yodel through the house while the rest of us spun our wheels getting ready. I think my parents were both naturally punctual, but my mother could get a group going far easier.

My parents almost never openly fought in front of us. And though I know that doesn't mean fights didn't happen, I felt that Josh and I also owed it to Zelda to not fight in front of her.

When Josh and I became parents, it exposed a deep weakness in our relationship. It probably does in everyone's, really, because a child presents a couple with the first true test of their ability to negotiate, to compromise, to make daily decisions, and to relent and to give in to another person sometimes. Buying a house and managing your way through a hair-raising mortgage process is *nothing* in comparison. Though Josh and I had taken on his personal characteristic of openly and sometimes hostilely attacking each other over, say, how good the films of Paul Thomas Anderson are, the stakes of so many of the arguments we'd had over the years before Zelda were extremely low.

The thing is that parenting is actually easier when you're on your own, without someone there to question the choices you're making. And since I was often the one alone with Zelda, I made many of the decisions myself.

To be clear, Josh wasn't an absentee father; he was simply a parent who worked a lot. There were plenty of times, thousands of hours, where it was the two of us together. And it was then that we fought for the first time over things that seemed to really matter. I found that I couldn't remain silent. I would correct his parenting or simply take over entirely. I found myself disagreeing openly with even small decisions he made.

He was not fond of this emerging tendency in me. I've always been a know-it-all corrector. This is not an attractive or good quality, and I sometimes try very hard to keep my thoughts to myself. But as I'd lay in bed at night with the baby monitor humming beside me, being hard on myself for the way I'd treated him during that day, for saying, "Don't make a big deal if she cries," or, "Don't turn the heat on now, it will wake her," I'd often come back around to the other side in my internal dialogue. "Wait a minute," I'd say. "He's the whole reason I'm so disagreeable to begin with! He's the one who showed me that speaking my mind was the best policy."

We had this argument out loud occasionally, too. "You're the reason I am this way now. I was much easier before," I'd say unhelpfully. If there was a shred of truth to it, what good did it do me to say it aloud? And so, the circular way of thinking completed itself and began anew.

We agreed on most things. We were politically aligned. We usually liked the same TV shows. Our temperaments worked well together. But parenting is a crazy test of a relationship. I can't say we did better than other people. But we didn't judge ourselves too harshly, and, ultimately, we sort of came to an agreement.

I won most of the arguments. We basically did and still do most of the parenting the way that I want to. That doesn't mean

I'm always right. I'm wrong sometimes even if it's hard for me to admit. And though Josh is naturally disagreeable, he is not a grudge keeper. In that first year or so of Zelda's life, he extended to me a great charity in not holding too much against me.

At home, my mother was the "cool parent." I wanted to emulate that much of her. I wanted to be cool. I think of myself as a cool person with good ideas. I know that's a funny way to want to be perceived, but it's true. I wanted Zelda to think of me as a cool mother. My father was firmer and in some ways more fear-inducing to me. If he said, "Go clean up your room," I did. With my mother, I could often negotiate. "Come help me?" I'd ask. She didn't always say yes, but I at least felt comfortable, and entitled, to ask.

But I was soon taken aback by the realization that Josh was the cool parent in Zelda's life, especially once she began to talk. "Daddy," she'd say when I asked who she wanted to read her stories at night. It didn't matter that she seemed to prefer him sometimes simply because he was easier to manipulate. I'd leave the room, letting him read, and then stand in the kitchen seething as I heard her stretch bedtime by another twenty minutes. "I need to go potty," she'd say. "I'm thirsty," she'd say. "I need a tissue," she'd say, and he'd fall for it every time.

I wasn't angry with him over these things. Well, I was at first. But I've grown to accept this dynamic. I am the decider, like my mother was before me, but in that role I'm also unequivocally the boss. Zelda knows she can't fuck with me. She doesn't fear me; I've tried so hard to ensure that she doesn't fear me, and there are no signs that she does. But she does not disobey me very often. These days she simply says, "Okay, Mommy, two minutes more," when I tell her how long there is until dinner.

I respect and accept this. I don't need to be everything to Zelda. I don't need to be the cool parent. She has Josh for that.

When my parents separated, when I was getting ready to enter tenth grade, I was relieved. I'm not sure why, exactly, but I hoped that their separation would lead to my mother drinking less. That hope turned out to be, like many others, unfulfilled. At the time of the separation, with my oldest brother, David, already at college, we decided that my brothers and I would stay with my mother. We wanted to stay with our mother too, because, well, she was the cool parent. Over the years, and with her increased drinking, we knew we could slide under her radar easier than we could my father's. I remember once telling my dad I was going to the bus stop (which was at the end of our driveway and visible from any of the many windows at the front of our house) and then tried to sneak around the back of the house and through the backyard. The truth was that I had no intention of going to school that day: I was headed to Emily's. I don't know why my father was late going to work that morning; usually he left before I had to get on the bus. Either way, he was waiting at the back door for me as I tried to slip into the yard.

"What are you doing?" he asked.

"I missed the bus," I lied, poorly. "I'm walking to school now."

"I watched you watch the bus go by," he said. "Get in the car, I'll drive you to school."

You couldn't get shit past my dad. I realize now that that's how I am as a mother. But I will be the first to admit that I am uncool as a mother. I'm in charge. As Zelda says, "You're da boss."

If we'd never had children, I believe Josh and I would

probably never have been truly confronted with this need to learn how to make decisions together, how to relent or come to an agreement even if disagreement remains. You can't simply keep arguing forever when another person, the child, needs your answer now: someone either needs to come around or they need to allow the other person to win.

And I learned something else: my fear, based on my own experience, of Josh and me fighting in front of Zelda, was somewhat useless. Of course we argue in front of her. We don't yell at each other violently, but we are, I have accepted, disagreeable people. My fear of open confrontation has died very hard, and my fear of hurting my daughter has been washed away like sand on a beach, slowly over time: she's absorbed so easily into this little family of ours, Band-Aids and all. We are who we are. She chimes in when we argue with her own opinion more often than not. And it's so obvious she knows and is secure in how much we love her.

CHAPTER 8

. . .

My mother was raised by a very opinionated woman of the Great Depression. Raised by an alcoholic herself, my grandma Peg was in some ways an amazing woman. She was a working mother in the 1950s, an interior decorator and then, with my grandfather, the bookkeeper at their framing business. But as a mother and then as a grandmother, she was exacting, especially in matters of dress. For her, appearances mattered almost to the exclusion of everything else. Though my mother knew a lot of this was bullshit, she spent most of her life, as far as I can tell, trying to please her own mother and inevitably failing. I remember hearing my grandmother tell her she should lose a "few pounds" or that her hair color needed to be touched up at the roots. I'd hear her quiet, *tsk-tsk* voice: "Kathy, is that what you're wearing?"

I know what it's like to live with your mother's baggage. I don't know where my grandmother's baggage came from, and I do not blame her for my mother's alcoholism, but I do think that my mother tried to course correct her relationship with me based on what she probably saw as the shortcomings of her own mom. Don't we all? That manifested itself as an open and pretty honest relationship with me. We talked freely about sex and drugs, and she told me wonderful stories about her teenage years. One of her favorite things to talk about was how when she went to see the Doors and Jim Morrison touched her face. She was seventeen years old, and it was her first concert. I wasn't afraid of my mother the way that I think she was afraid of her own. My mother made me strong enough and smart enough to tell her when I found out that I was pregnant, and she was open enough to be able to listen to it. If that situation was difficult for her, as I've come to realize as a mother myself that it must have been, she herself never complained to me. And I think she certainly wanted to be better than her mother in this way. I never really felt that my mother had expectations of me that I would never be able to meet. Except for one thing.

With a baby and a little kid, it's easy to dress them. They wear what you put on them or, later, what you buy. I never thought about what was in my closet and my drawers very much, not for the first ten or twelve years of my life. So the fact that my three-and-a-half-year-old already has decidedly strong opinions about what she wants to wear shocked me, and it exposes her genetic predisposition to care.

I didn't care what I looked like, never felt put together right. I felt uncomfortable in my body and so, to counteract that, I eventually stopped caring completely. This irritated my mother, who had spent my childhood braiding my hair carefully and planning outfits for me. She prided herself on her own appearance and, by some extension, on mine. I hated shopping, though I loved that it was one of the few times my mother and I were out alone.

I grew up acutely aware that one of the major ways my

mother showed the world that she cared for me was in dressing me very well. Appearances mattered. She could break free from her mother and raise her daughter to be truthful and comfortable talking to her about the things that did matter, but she couldn't temper or hide her disappointment at the ever-increasingly apparent truth, which was that I was slovenly and what was still in the '90s called a "tomboy." She wasn't superficial, but despite her best intentions, she had internalized her mother's attitudes that appearances mattered.

When I was a child, my long hair was always clean and shiny and tangle-free. I never, ever wore pants as a baby. Even in toddlerhood, I remember going to bed with my hair in curlers and wearing tights and itchy, formal dresses with patent leather shoes to all occasions. To this day, family members still comment on how lovely I was dressed as a baby and child. I didn't mind her dressing me as she pleased. Until I did.

Nothing came between my mother and me fast approaching my teen years more than these same issues: what to wear, makeup, hair, shoes. It started, as most problems probably do for parents, around the end of middle school. And it *did* start out in a predictable direction: I decided first that I wanted to wear heavy makeup—black eyeliner, dark red lipstick, and black clothing. It was a Goth phase. My mother was a good old Catholic schoolgirl, so she understood my need to rebel to some extent. I think she thought of it as a Madonna-inspired expression of my inner rage, and she was right.

But in middle school I couldn't find any evidence that there were cool things outside of whatever shit was on TV and in magazines. To me, alternative music was, like, the Smiths or the Cure, and even that stuff was on MTV, if late at night.

My mom stayed up with me on Sundays to watch *120 Minutes*, so, I reasoned, how weird could it possibly be? My *mother* watched it.

She was very tolerant even of my emerging desire to wear Revlon Red lipstick in ninth grade, when there were very few high schoolers doing such a thing. Though I'd had my ears pierced the first time with my grandma Peg at the mall on my fifth birthday, the next rounds were carried out by my mom in the basement of our house while watching MTV late on a Sunday night. She iced my ears and did it with a needle and a thread and a potato, like they did back when she was a teenager, she said. She was sometimes really cool.

But by the time I was in high school, my ideas changed quickly about what was attractive, about what I wanted to look like, and about what I wanted to wear. My mother indulged me when I requested to have my waist-length hair cut off. She allowed me to go to a barber on my own after school, with a picture I'd found in a magazine of a woman with short hair. I think it might have been Demi Moore. Girls with very short hair weren't that common then; this was years before the mainstreaming of the pixie cut. No one I went to school with had short hair. My mother gave me the money to pay for the haircut. And to her credit, she did not freak out about it, although it was much shorter than she had expected. I told the barber, "Keep cutting," over and over until the hair looked as though I wouldn't need to fuck with it or style it anymore. And once I cut my hair, I never wanted it to grow long again. I dutifully went to get it cut every six to eight weeks, and she dutifully said nothing.

My mother also didn't say much when I stopped wearing makeup and jewelry. She didn't say much when I began to only wear black and white, mostly my grandfather's old clothes that my grandma Elly had given me when she'd cleaned out his closets after he died.

But eventually, when confronted with my whole look, it proved to be a bit much for her, and she started to make little comments and suggestions that, needless to say, I didn't take kindly to. My new aesthetic gave me something I'd never had before: confidence. I felt all right carrying myself, my body, around the halls of the high school. I felt, if not attractive to others, at least satisfied with myself.

Like my mother with her own mother, I never wanted anything other than approval. And like my mother, I seemed suddenly, somehow, incapable of getting it. It's incredibly destabilizing to discover that what has given you confidence for the first time in your new, adult body is also causing your mother pain. But instead of trying to change myself to please her, as she did with her own mother, I went in the opposite direction and decided to please only myself. I decided, then and there, that no one would ever make me feel bad about myself physically.

I look at the photos of myself from then, and I sort of see why she was unhappy. I was a thin girl in what were widely considered to be men's clothes then, no makeup, short hair. No jewelry. I was her only daughter, and she'd shown me, by example her whole life, what it meant to be a woman who cared for herself. I was mostly clean, but I stopped shaving my legs and I stopped worrying. For me, it was freedom. For her, it was disappointment. And she didn't hide it well. "I already have three sons," she snapped at me once when she found that I'd replaced all my underwear with men's briefs.

The freedom to not give a shit about what other people

think of your looks is just that: it was liberating on a level not previously experienced by me, teen Laura. Some days I felt like running through the halls or up the hill behind the school to where my old elementary school was. If I ran long enough, I would eventually hit the path that carried me into my neighborhood and home. I felt almost like a kid again.

I sometimes wish that my mother could have learned from me, a little of my ability to not give a shit with regards to her *own* mother. I know it doesn't work that way: she created in me that ability, but still, she could have used some of it herself. She could have benefited greatly from the ability to say to her mother, "Yes, this is what I'm wearing. Do you have a problem with that?" as I said to her. As I grew up, I occasionally felt the urge to defend my mother against her own mother.

But I often wonder now why it was that my mother, an adult, seemed so defenseless against her own mother, when I was perfectly capable as a teenager of standing up to mine.

Mothers and daughters, even ones not dealing with divorce and alcoholism, always have a falling-out point. I know this because every friend I had was fighting with her own mother at the exact same time as I was. There was a lot of sighing and eye rolling. My father didn't seem to know what to do with the new me, the one who wasn't comforted by ice cream or a shopping trip or a hug. He backed off, as I'm sure many fathers of teenage girls before him had. But my mother thought—rightfully, I'm sure—that she understood what I was going through.

She didn't. I soon realized that my mother had never felt what I felt. She never rebelled, and if she ever felt reason to, she didn't admit it to me. She was a "popular" and beautiful, blond-haired girl in high school. I was uninterested in being popular.

My mother, who I thought of as progressive and smart, was not pleased at this prospect of the new me. She was even more sheltered than I was there in the suburbs. She'd never lived on her own, she'd never been out in the world or lived in a big city. I knew that I was disappointing her, but it also seemed like a superficial argument. It seemed like the fight about my clothes was a battle we were having because we couldn't fight about what was actually wrong in our relationship. We were talking around the real problem: she was an alcoholic. And once my father had moved out, that fact was front and center. She drank more, more often, and more openly. My brothers stopped going to school some days. I was often late or absent myself, preferring to leave school early to smoke cigarettes. I took to simply walking out of the high school whenever I damn well pleased.

This led to countless long Saturday detentions, where I was tasked with watering plants or shelving books. One Saturday that I remember was the day after Richard Nixon died. Emily and I were assigned to create a memorial for the ex-president in the display case outside the library. "Farewell, Dick," the display case read in those tacked-up paper cutout letters schools always have, surviving long enough into Monday for students to see it, resulting in yet another detention.

My mom seemed only somewhat aware of my dire circumstances. Mostly, I kept things to myself and still managed to have a pretty good time. I wasn't actually failing out of school, just floating along, doing the least amount of work possible.

What my mom did care about openly was my appearance.

It stood in for so much in our relationship at that time. She thought the fact that I didn't care meant something, that it was a commentary on or a reaction against her.

At the time, I thought that what I was wearing had nothing to do with her, but now, I'm not so sure she wasn't right after all. Now, I wonder if I wasn't making a statement to hurt her.

When I found out that I was in fact going to have a girl, I simply wanted for my daughter to be herself. Two thousand fourteen was hundreds, thousands of miles away from the mid-1990s. Zelda wouldn't have to argue about if she could have short hair as she grew up, because it's not as big of a deal; there are more women with short hair now than there were then.

The world into which Zelda would be born was a lot different, as worlds often are about dressing trends. Though I was sure she would eventually find something to irritate her aging mother with, I dedicated myself to the concept that I would never, ever make her feel bad about her appearance. Though my mother never made me feel shame about my body the way her own mother had about weight or diet, she had left me with a bad taste in my mouth about all manners of things dress-related, so much so that, to this day, when I step into a pair of shoes with heels and a dress, I feel the anger of resentment bubbling up inside me. Even when I like the way that I look in traditionally female clothing, I am angry and uncomfortable.

What I guess I didn't consider was that once I did find out I was having a girl, I might want to dress her like one. I don't so much mean "buy pink," because I'm a lover of all colors, even the ones that are stereotypically gendered. I don't hold anything against pink.

No, I mean that I was surprised to find, almost immediately, that I wanted to buy my unborn fetus dresses. Frilly ones. Patent leather shoes. White tights with lace on the butt. Just like my mother had for me. I didn't know if Zelda would be my only child, but I'd waited a long time for her, and I was overjoyed to be having a girl. I didn't expect, though, to want to buy her dresses.

But I did. I wanted to do this very badly, and I felt almost ashamed to acknowledge it, after my years of talking about the patriarchy's rules for dress. I'd raged against this machine so hard. What did it mean to so suddenly want to be inside that machine?

I keep a lot of things to myself. Plenty of people who have known me for years never heard me utter the word "alcoholic" when talking about my mother. But I was not and really never have been shy when it comes to the topic of dress: in this one area, I admit, I have slandered my mother's good name for full effect, trying to drum up sympathy wherever I could.

She scarred me for sure, though I admit freely that the scars from arguing over whether I should wear men's briefs or shave my legs were pretty superficial. I see now that, to some extent, my years of telling and retelling, shaping the narrative of the Big Fights my mother and I had over clothes, was a comedy.

I think I did it because it was a story that could have come from any mother-daughter relationship. It was one of the very few falling-outs I ever had with her that was, well, normal. It was a very typical "mom story," and I didn't have very many of those.

Thinking of it this way makes me sad even now. Knowing that I grasped every day for mundane stories to tell about my mother so that I would have things in common with the armies of disaffected daughters out there is very sad. I didn't want to tell people that my mother sometimes berated me incoherently in the dark as I just tried to go to sleep, or that later, when I was nearly an adult but still living with her, she once went out "for a walk, to buy stamps" and then didn't come home for two days. I didn't want to tell people about my mother taking me for an abortion. I didn't want to tell them about her sickness.

Because even though there are millions of people just like me out there, with mothers who love them despite their addictions, or people who have it far worse, what I found myself wanting more than anything when I thought of my mother was simply to have things be "normal." For a person who has always, always prided herself on her lack of normalcy as I have, this is not an easy thing to admit.

So I complained unendingly about my mother's old-school ways of thinking about people's looks. I rolled my eyes at her as the years wore on, even though I came closer to understanding her disappointment as I thought about having my own child. I softened my attitude toward her as I sat on my growing, pregnant ass staring at a computer screen, thinking about buying my daughter dresses from Nordstrom.

For I could see already that I wanted to shower her with the best that I could afford and offer. Not just materially but as a blanket policy.

And once she was born, indeed, I found true pleasure in dressing her. In the alternate reality in which I now lived, I cared about clothing and planned outfits a day in advance.

Special occasions and holidays always demanded special care. I washed her hair—of which there was perilously little to start—with special shampoo and brushed it gently. I thought about piercing her ears, though I never did. Like every other parent, I filed her tiny, translucent fingernails.

I knew then and know now that I was not special in any of this. But though I always expected to love my daughter, I did not expect to feel so invested in her physical form. Because I mentally shrugged when I looked at myself in the mirror, I very much expected to feel the same about her corporal body.

"I don't care if she's ugly or not," I said aloud to friends when I was pregnant, and I meant it. Of course I meant it: whether we are "beautiful" or not doesn't matter at all; it never mattered to me.

But I was presented with her physical beauty from the first minute. She was perfect. Her skin was smooth and clear; her eyes were full of joy and fringed by impossibly long eyelashes; her nose was the best-shaped nose I'd ever seen. Everything about her was beautiful.

I'm sure every parent marvels this way; it's our right to do so. But seeing and loving my daughter's actual body was my first experience of really caring about something so physical that I wanted to groom and shop for it. I wanted, in short, what my mother had almost certainly wanted for me.

I abandoned my caution. She was too young to decide what she wanted to wear, so I was in charge. Eventually (sooner than I thought, actually), she'd have ideas of her own that I would respect, but until she did, I would not feel guilty about what I dressed her in.

I spent a lot of Zelda's early life shopping on my computer or my phone and in stores. Though I did often favor what I would call "genderless" clothing—onesies and jumpsuits and pants that any baby could wear—I also found that yeah, I definitely liked dressing her in jumpers and dresses and "girly" clothing.

I found that practical concerns often trumped aesthetic ones, so Zelda wore many kimono and legging combos. She wore a lot of leisure wear. A lot of one-piece ensembles. I found myself becoming surer every day among the racks of clothing in stores, and, for the first time in my life, I enjoyed shopping. Almost.

I was occasionally weighed down with the memory of shopping with my own mother. Can any activity be more boring to a child than clothes shopping? Only the countless hours I spent sitting silently in church and catechism class could beat out the hours spent shopping, sitting in a cart or beside a stroller bearing my brother or, worst of all, walking. Nothing, nothing could make me forget the sensation of burning eyes from the fluorescent lights of shopping mall department stores, my own personal Vegas-style hell where there are no windows and there are no clocks. I wandered, with a dry mouth, noiselessly through the racks, not allowed to explore very far, nor allowed to touch anything, nor allowed to even speak too loudly.

During these early shopping trips with Zelda, who was more often than not strapped to my chest in a baby carrier, blissfully unaware of her dire shopping circumstances, I was sometimes overwhelmed with my sense that what I was now enjoying had dogged me for most of my life. It's good to relearn sometimes. Sometimes we can change.

*　*　*

I don't know what Zelda will end up looking like. When I return to the photos of her from six months or a year and a half ago, there is deep recognition and familiarity there, even though she has changed so much. I recognize in the short videos of her baby mumblings the sound that ultimately became her current speaking voice, and I see in her past faces the face she now has, more formed and solid, more human than to start.

I stand by my long-held belief that looks aren't very important. That love and attraction and affection are based on other things. My daughter's personality is far and away the best thing about her. The way she reaches up out of her crib at night while she lays on her back, drinking her milk, her wide eyes dozing off, to touch my hand. I know her mannerisms and emotions and tics better than I really ever thought I would know anyone. It's an incredible joy to know her and an incredible journey to watch her become herself.

In this way, I have come to respect and sympathize more with my mother, though I still believe she chose the wrong battle. Why it mattered to her wasn't in her control: she was simply going on what her own mother had taught her. That self-respect could be found in the way one clothed their body is not in fact untrue. It's just that it's also possible to have self-respect and *not* care about clothes or how you look. I know; I'm living proof! I'm almost forty and I still don't give a shit how I look beyond being clean and sort of well-groomed. I don't care if my socks match or if my pants are torn. I don't really know my dress size.

One Saturday morning when I was in high school, probably hungover, I was eating a giant plate of fried eggs and toast with butter, shoveling the food in like I'd been starved for days, though I never missed a meal.

"Someday you'll regret eating that way," she said, sounding like a mother straight out of *The Group*. I hadn't read *The Group* yet and didn't even know who Mary McCarthy was. "I've never lived a day in my life not watching what I eat."

I looked up at her, stunned. What did she mean? Had she been dieting all this time, all my life, and I'd never noticed?

Kids are fucking myopic, and my mother kept her secrets close. If she was dieting all the time, she never told anyone that I know of. She didn't keep a notebook or something, the way that I would after Zelda was born, trying to lose ten pounds for the better part of a year.

"What do you mean?" I asked, mentally trying to go back in time over all the things I'd ever seen her eat. Did my mother eat? Of course.

I'd seen her sit on the couch eating sleeves of Saltines. I knew that she liked BLTs and didn't really like cheese. She liked cottage cheese, black tea, canned tuna fish, dry toast, hard-boiled eggs, and grapefruits. She liked, I realize now, what I can only call " '80s diet food for women." Loved it. Or did she? Did she simply avoid eating most things because she didn't want to get fat? Did people live that way?

"You'll regret eating like that because you're not teaching yourself to moderate. You won't always have your father's metabolism."

That turned the conversation. I didn't want to get into some weird, upsetting conversation that circled into "your father" territory with her.

But I thought of this conversation a lot after Zelda was born. It was, if I recall, the only direct conversation the two of us ever had about dieting, but, more important, I snapped out of my oblivion.

It wasn't just the teenage girls I knew who ate candy and spit it out, not wanting to ingest the calories: it was all women. If my own mother had been watching what she ate for her entire life, what was I supposed to be doing?

My teenage self rejected her concern. But after Zelda was born, I realized that my mother had four kids and remained very thin. I got sort of fat from one baby. What would four do to my body? And as someone who cared deeply about how she was seen, how did she process that?

I didn't worry too much or rush to lose the weight, although I did briefly consider the completely demoralizing prospect of buying a food scale. I was still fairly stubbornly confident, even if my body seemed so changed. But I do feel differently about some of those conversations I had with my mother. I hope to learn from them, to not repeat them with my own daughter. But, in the past few years of learning what it's like to actually care and be responsible for another person's body entirely, I understand completely how the illusion of ownership can arise.

I don't kid myself that I own Zelda. But I want to teach her to truly own herself.

CHAPTER 9

• • •

The true start of my teenager-dom was in the summer of
1992, when Emily, Vanessa, Ellen, and I got dropped off
at an outdoor amphitheater twenty miles from home that was
that day hosting Lollapalooza. It was the first time I remember really being allowed to go somewhere alone for basically
an entire day with my friends. Ellen's father drove us the
forty-five minutes to the venue, dropped us off, and said, "I'll
see you back here at eleven thirty tonight, get out." It was
11:00 in the morning. Twelve-plus hours alone with my
friends in a giant crowd was unimaginable freedom.

We were there to see a dizzying array of bands that included the Red Hot Chili Peppers, Pearl Jam, Soundgarden,
Ice-T, the Jesus and Mary Chain, and Ministry. It was a real
'90s cornucopia. I was there primarily to see Ministry. This
was the beginning of the Goth Laura phase and only a few
months before that phase dipped into the androgynous-bad-
dresser-fighting-with-her-mom phase. The first band that
played that day was a British band called Lush. Lush was led
by two women, one of whom had flame-red hair. I'd never
heard of them before, and I'd never heard music like that in

my life. I fell in love instantly, and that day, mostly because of that band, changed my life.

People tell you that singing can calm a baby. That makes sense: music has always calmed me. And Zelda wasn't alive very long before we attempted to use music to relax her. Unfortunately, we were, while still in the hospital just twelve or fifteen hours after she was born, limited in what we could offer her. I wish that the first piece of music Zelda ever heard was not "Work" by Iggy Azalea. But it was. It is. The first piece of music she ever heard was "Work." I even wrote this fact down in her baby book: "First song I ever heard: 'Work,' by Iggy Azalea, played on a phone."

We played it for her, not on the day she was born but the day after, because it was the only song that Josh had actually downloaded to his phone and we were still in the hospital, and the Wi-Fi was spotty. I say this as a way of excusing us, maybe, but it's true. We played her what was on hand. It was an Iggy Azalea song.

I wish I could take it back because now it is one of those songs that, though it may never be "special" to Zelda—since really, I'd have to tell her this fact for her to even know it—it will always, somehow and so improbably, be special to me. And I hate the song "Work." It's not good. It's crass, and not even crass in a good way. Not crass in the way that I'm crass. Crass like bad crass. "I've been up all night, tryna get that rich / I've been work work work work working on my shit."

The last time I heard "Work," probably three months ago at random, I was sitting in a parking lot in my car, waiting to pick someone up from a train. I burst into tears. I was probably suffering from PMS, or maybe something else had gone awry that day. I can't remember the details, only the fact that Iggy Azalea's "Work" made me burst into tears once late last year as I sat alone in my car. I don't randomly cry, and even though music often does overwhelm me to tears, "Work" surprised me. But I cried that day because even though I hate the song, it's the first song that my daughter ever heard, and it triggers inside of me a deep feeling of remembrance and loss, as well as a happiness so great I sometimes feel like clawing us back into that hospital room.

When Zelda heard music for the first time, she was laying in that plastic salad bin they give you at the hospital to contain the baby. For the first hours of her life, she lay in that clear plastic container on a steel inclined gurney that had squeaky wheels. I could barely stand from the incision in my gut, but I felt like another woman, a woman not me. I felt superhuman. I could stay awake for the rest of her life, sitting beside her, simply to ensure her survival. All thoughts of my own safety and happiness had, for the moment, departed. I don't re-member what the second, third, or fourth songs that Zelda heard were. I remember only the first.

I'd love to be able to say, "the first music my daughter heard was the sweet, clear-as-a-bell sound of her mother's voice, softly purring 'Edelweiss.' " Tough shit.

I have always sung to Zelda. "Work" is the only musical mistake I am willing to own up to. Because I clung to habit and routine early in her life, I quickly developed a set list and simply stuck with it, adding a song every now and then. The standards of our early list included "Frère Jacques," "The Itsy Bitsy Spider," "Alligator" by Tegan & Sara, and "Don't Shake Your Baby" by me. I wrote it one day when I realized that, contrary to all the terrifying subway ads warning against shaking my baby, my baby wanted nothing more in this world than to be shaken, albeit lightly. She thought shaking was fucking hilarious. "Don't shake, don't shake your baby. Don't shake, don't shake your baby. Don't shake, don't shake your baby: Just kidding, shake your baby." Instant classic.

But though we added to the repertoire slowly, I played for her all the music I myself wanted to hear each day. Like the books I read to her, I didn't limit myself to kid's music, because like her opinions on clothes, she was, at first, too young to voice them. So we listened to Pavement and Air and the Breeders and the Beach Boys. Why not?

Zelda showed interest in music very early on. So much so that the first thing she did upon learning to sit up was to start dancing, sitting in the middle of her bedroom floor, just jiggling away. Before she learned to crawl, Zelda learned to dance. I don't know if all babies dance, but Zelda always did. It was essential to her being, and it was an overwhelming joy to see her ingest the music, to see her body relent, relax, and go with it. For her, music and dancing were intrinsically linked, especially before she had words.

When Zelda was less than a year old, I rented the 1982 movie *Annie* on iTunes and showed it to her. It did not go very well. She was unaccustomed at that age to television, because I took the American Academy of Pediatrics (AAP) recommendations to heart, and her nanny, who cared for her as I started to get back to writing, didn't watch TV, either. Kids under two, the AAP told me, should not view "screens." At all.

Luckily, Josh and I only ever watched TV at night, long past her 7:30 p.m. bedtime, so the most she ever saw in her first two years of life was a few minutes of an old episode of *Sesame Street* thrown on in a panic so I could shove some food in my face or boil water for dinner.

I realized in the maybe ten minutes that we watched that day that *Annie* was scarier than I remembered. I had forgotten everything but the songs, probably because I had only ever seen it a few times. VCRs weren't that common when I was very young, so I knew the story from a book and the soundtrack. I barely remembered how menacing the actual movie was. In *Annie*, basically all the adults are horrifying and terrible (except for Grace Farrell, of course, who is resplendent and beautiful and perfect). Miss Hannigan, played by Carol Burnett (who is magical) is a mean drunk. Daddy Warbucks is a child-hating Republican; Rooster and Lily are actual criminals. There are dog catchers and policemen. Even the orphans, who have, admittedly, been living a hard-knock life, are rough and mean. Annie's progress through the narrative is one of near-constant stress and danger, and Annie herself often rejects the easier path to comfort and happiness in favor of the harder but more authentic path. I saw this really clearly as an adult where before, as a kid, I simply wanted to be an orphan.

I tried *Annie* again when Zelda was nearing her third birthday. My timing could not have been better: within one viewing, she was hooked. The movie is still too scary for her— we have to fast-forward through Annie hanging off the bridge or there will be tears—but the emotional center of Annie's life is not lost on Zelda. Nor are the show tunes. "It's the Hard Knock Life" is what Zelda calls a "group song," where all the kids in the movie sing together. Another of her favorite examples of a group song is "Do Re Mi," from *The Sound of Music*. *Annie* perfectly combines Zelda's first two loves in life:

performative cleaning (something she started to do as soon as she could walk) and song and dance routines. When she began to choreograph "It's the Hard Knock Life" for herself in our living room, she needed only to run a few paces away to grab her little cleaning kit, complete with rags, sponges, mops, and a bucket.

I wanted to pass on my love of music to Zelda the same way I wanted her to love books, not because I wanted her to be more like me—I don't. I have spent much of my life anxious and tortured on behalf of other people, and I don't want that for her. But music and reading have always been great refuges to me, mental spaces that are wide and clear and open, untroubled and never ending. When I was an upset teenager, having just argued with my mother or my boyfriend, when I wanted to smash something against a wall just to see things broken, I often crawled into the closet in my bedroom, where I would sit listening to music and drawing on the walls. It was quiet and dark in there; I kept boxes of candles and cigarettes. The thought of the dual fire hazard of smoking and candles in a thin 1960s suburban closet space, the thought of the smell alone, makes me want to wretch now, but that's what I did. I hid there or lay under the blankets of my bed, reading books and listening to rock music.

And if I was not yet able to imagine myself in other places or in other situations, if I hadn't yet thought out what I might like to "do" next, once I graduated from high school, it was reading and music that transported me elsewhere first. And so it was that in a very important way, I was a normal American suburban teenager, dreaming away the extra hours through a boombox CD player.

I should admit that music, even sort of bad but beloved music, has always had the power to make me cry spontaneously. Usually it is not such a disastrous arrangement as "Work," but still, I have cried listening to the strains of Neil Diamond or ABBA, to Madonna and to Mastodon. I have cried at more live shows than I can count. I remember crying at Le Tigre and Gossip. At Fleet Foxes and the Walkmen. I cried onstage when my own band played, and I cried in the audiences of tiny smoky bars when my brothers' and boyfriends' bands played. I have always, always been the person wiping my eyes standing in the middle of a venue.

In childhood I clung to my records and tapes, graduating to CDs around middle school. I wore them out and wore them in. I memorized breathing patterns and beat drops. Hand claps and snare hits. I was never a casual consumer of music. I listened with an ear bent on mimicry and memorization. Music was serious business to me, and I studied it, even before I could read.

It was also overwhelmingly emotional. I thought—still think—that if I listen hard enough for a certain amount of time, my ears will stop straining and I'll be able to simply absorb it. The lyrics will wash over me and I won't have to work at it anymore.

There are so many records that I know in this intimate, listened-to-them-literally-thousands-of-times way.

The soundtrack to the movie *Annie* was probably my first musical obsession. It's also the first movie I ever saw in a movie theater, with Peg, my mother's mother, who took me for an Orange Julius afterward and bought me a new dress. I was almost but not quite five, but I remember gripping the chair in the theater, transfixed and terrified by the movie. I wanted, like so many other girls wanted, to be an orphan.

Back then, you couldn't just watch a movie whenever you wanted to: that technology simply didn't exist yet. Eventually, I did get a VHS copy of *Annie*, but even that system was precarious. The tape had only so many views in it. VHS tapes were sort of expensive at the time, so you couldn't waste precious viewing life on fast-forwarding to the beginning of "It's the Hard Knock Life," the best song and dance number of the movie, over and over. No, when I sat down to watch the movie, I usually watched it from start to finish.

I had the vinyl record of the soundtrack when I wanted to indulge my compulsive, repetitive desires. I still remember the exact sound of the crackly dead air and how long it lasted between the end of the song "Tomorrow" and the beginning of "It's the Hard Knock Life." I had long enough to go from a sitting ("Tomorrow") to a standing position in my bedroom, which was small and mostly filled by my bed. For listening, I wedged myself between the bed and the wall, on the farthest side of the room, so that, if the door to my room opened and I was sitting on the other side of the bed, I couldn't be seen. The carpeting in my room for most of my childhood was a purplish color, and it was worn thin in places, making it very uncomfortable to lay on. If I lay there silently, with my ear to the ground near the heating vent, I could hear as clear as a bell the conversations my brothers were having in the bedroom that they shared in the basement.

I spent so many hours alone in that room, studying the songs from *Annie*. And when, around the second grade, I made friends and simultaneously discovered MTV and Michael Jackson and Madonna, I never fully discarded my love for

Annie. I still had the records as a teenager, sitting inside my closet, unlistened to but not gotten rid of, either.

My parents always listened to music, too. My father called most of the shots there, preferring oldies from the '50s and early '60s, doo-wop, and early rock. But he also, like so many Polish Pittsburghers, listened to a lot of polka music, and we spent a ton of time going to polka dances all over the place when I was a kid. As I aged, I grew to feel some embarrassment about these weekend activities when I realized that most of the kids I went to school with didn't go to polka dances.

In the 1980s, I graduated from children's music to adult, like every other kid on the planet, at around the time I started school. I eventually flirted with heavy metal, and for a long time, like many girls my age, I blew with the wind: whatever the boys were listening to, I listened to. Ozzy Osbourne? Sure, okay. King Diamond? Hell, why not?

But in the summer of 1992, I found the things that seemed to be made for me in music. They were women. I still loved Madonna, but increasingly I felt that she was more of a product than a musical outlet for me. I wanted Sonic Youth and Lush and Belly and the Breeders. I wanted to hear women actually making the music, holding the instruments, writing the songs. It helped, of course, that these women were beautiful in the new mold that I wanted to be beautiful in: they were sort of weird. They were feminists, though I didn't use that word yet.

I wanted Liz Phair, the only artist I have ever heard my mother say unequivocally that she "hated." She hated her voice and the words she said with that voice. I loved Liz even more for offending my mother.

My parents always had the radio on. Our house must have

been so loud. My brothers had their music too, but I hid away in my room, studying my own.

My mother was cool, almost completely due to the fact that she was twenty-four years old when I was born. I was thirty-six when Zelda was born: my mother liked most of the same music I liked, and I still think of myself as cool to some degree. But I suspect by the time she is a teenager, I won't be cool enough to like whatever music Zelda likes. I'll be an old-ass bitch by the time Zelda is asking me to take her to shows or whatever zany shit she'll be up to in the ninth or tenth grade, existing in that weird zone between child and adulthood, where you can still tolerate the tolerable parents and you still need rides all the time.

◆　◆　◆

I didn't feel like we lived in the actual world. American suburbs hold a really special place in my heart. There's something very kooky and cute about them that I love, but where we lived, where I grew up, going to the grocery store or pharmacy in the only strip mall in town was about as much excitement as one could expect from a weeknight.

There were buses that you could grab to get to the actual city of Pittsburgh; the trip took about an hour, and my mother would have killed me if I'd ever attempted such a thing. I didn't: it seemed like far too much effort even though by then the city, any city, was a draw to me.

And we would use any excuse to get there. In tenth grade, Ellen and I signed on to a huge walk to benefit multiple sclerosis one fall and came in dead last out of hundreds of participants. We walked slowly around different distinct parts of the city, stopping in shops to buy incense or get coffee.

"How do these look?" Ellen asked me, trying on a pair of Doc Martens at the Airwair store. "Do you think we're allowed to just shop during the walk?" I asked. I was always the one to worry, just a little.

What I did not have, in any form, was a plan for what I was going to do after high school. Unlike Emily and Vanessa and Ellen, who all had parents who were pushing them to go to college, to study for the SATs, my parents were simply trying to hold things together, hold disaster back at every turn. I hadn't failed any grades or been held back, but I was just floating by on my good nature and my aptitude. My older brother, David, was the only one of us who received any of the traditional "Well, now it's time to apply for college" talks from my parents. He'd shipped off to the University of Pittsburgh and was doing whatever he was doing, while I was making do.

And in the space left empty by my parents' separation and my father's moving, there was a lot of darkness. My dad took my brothers on weekends and was incessantly checking up on us, but he'd left physically, and one of the things about an alcoholic family is, once somebody leaves, they're out. David, and to a great extent my father, was forced outside the circle when he physically departed. My dad was only twenty minutes away, but that didn't matter. My brothers and I lied to him a great deal about what was going on at home.

I'd like to say that this was simple denial on my part, but really, it was quite selfish. Now that I was a teenager, it was fairly convenient for me to have just one parent around, especially one who was ill-equipped to wrangle me. I could, to put it bluntly, do whatever the fuck I wanted. As I said, my mother was a cool mom and was so much easier to live with simply because she was not paying as much attention.

I worried and made sure that my mother grocery shopped, and I tried to clean up around the house, but in reality, things fell apart pretty quickly, and home became a place where most of us never were. I didn't know what my mother was doing most of the time, and often, if I needed to talk to her, I'd simply call down the street to the bar where I knew she usually was. My grandparents were closed off from this, too. My grandma Peg had never been great at dealing with reality, and around the time that my parents separated, my grandfather was diagnosed with Alzheimer's. He wasn't even seventy years old. It progressed quickly, and she had her hands very full with him.

So it was that I found, somehow, an upside to my mother's alcoholism. Surely I'd have given anything for stability and a mother who was reliable and honest and nice, but in the absence of that, I made due with freedom. I had come by it honestly: I didn't need to hide anything from my parents or sneak around. I simply had a mother who suddenly allowed me to do pretty much anything that I wanted. Luckily, my desires were mostly legal, mostly safe, and mostly harmless.

Increasingly, I felt more isolated than even before. I'd been isolated my whole life, often by choice. But now, I felt true division away from everyone and everything. I didn't really feel as though I could trust anyone at all: my parents, my brothers, my grandparents, my friends. I had a few teachers I confided in piecemeal, but largely my adult world was very sparsely populated and quiet.

I remember from that period the sound my school locker door made when I slammed it shut, and there was nobody— not a soul—in the hallway besides me. I smoked in the bathroom outside the school library, the same library that I loved and hid in, warm paneled with windows backing onto a courtyard. I still have dreams that I am cutting class, walking through the empty, tired afternoon halls, or falling asleep in the back of the darkened auditorium, where I had theater classes and often watched movies once a week to end the day.

I remember these hiding places, where I went with friends but just as often alone. I remember getting caught smoking in that library bathroom, the last time I ever smoked in it, with Ellen. All that time we'd smoked in there, never knowing that the handicapped stall, which we had commandeered for our very own, shared a common wall with the librarian's office. The vent in the bathroom blew air into her office, and so she wandered over to us in that bathroom to let us know that the smoke had billowed into her office. She told us to go straight to the principal's office but never followed up on our progress there, so we simply left school for the day.

I wandered around on my own a lot, thinking but coming up with no answers. I usually ended up with my friends or a boy I was interested in, but much of the time it took me hours to get there. I formed habits that I still struggle to support, so antithetical are they to being a social animal. I require hours of prep time before social events, and I want so much time to myself. "I can't think," I say, when I don't get it. I need a completely empty house sometimes to write a piece, often avoiding the work for days, then vomiting it out in the space of an hour or two when I suddenly find myself alone.

It was then, when I was sixteen, seventeen years old, that I became who I have remained. A person who saw herself motherless, even though I was not. I grew upward and outward, expanding and sloughing off the extra pieces. I felt unsure of most things and didn't know what I wanted to do with my life.

I'm convinced anyway that no teenager should know what they want to do when they're in high school, but maybe that's simply convenient for me to think, since I didn't know anything about that yet. I didn't even properly think that I wanted to escape my parents. I guess I simply would have been happy to go on attending high school. I wasn't ready to be finished with it all yet. But the end of my official childhood was fast approaching, and I did not have any choice in the matter.

In hindsight, I'm tempted to say that I didn't really have much of a childhood beyond the age of seven or eight, mostly because of my mother's alcoholism. I felt so conflicted about her. I loved her so much, but she also was my greatest—really my only—source of pain. I have always wondered what I would have turned out like in the absence of her problems, and though I am wary of making direct connections, pulled tight like a string, from one parent to another, Zelda has provided me with some indication that often children are simply born very serious. Though she has a great capacity for humor, she too, like both of her parents, seems born for work. She's never really played with toys, and when we buy her a toy version of some real-life object—a phone, a computer, a watering can—she often rejects it for the real, adult one. If my personality, anxious and serious and exacting, is not wholly the product of my mother's alcoholism, well, that makes sense to me. But it's surprising to me to see the way that traits transfer to a new person.

A true love of music works in both directions: rather than my simply passing on my love of certain records or artists to Zelda, almost immediately she also passed some on to me. In the earliest months of her life, Josh and I began looking for a new house outside the city, a little up in the suburbs of New

York City. As I'd aged and now as I'd become a mother, suddenly the prospect of such a move, despite my lifelong despair at the prospect of suburbs, became increasingly attractive to me. But when Zelda was just born, house hunting became a casual fun activity for a Saturday or Sunday morning. Every other weekend or so we'd go out and look at one house. Zelda was a city baby and unaccustomed to riding in cars, and so we made a habit early on of playing her the same quiet and calming album every time we got in the car, Lorde's *Pure Heroine*. Josh was a huge fan of the record, but I was more suspicious of it. I didn't like something about it; it hadn't grabbed me on first listen. Some records, even brilliant ones, take some warming up to.

But Zelda seemed to like it, and so every time we got in the car, we'd throw on *Pure Heroine* until eventually it was the only album we played if we wanted her to take a nap. I've listened to *Pure Heroine* probably more than any other record of my adult life and, over the months, it grew on me until I came to consider it one of the best albums I've ever heard. Thanks to Josh and Zelda, I have Lorde. Sometimes, your best discoveries come from other people, and there's almost nothing more satisfying than when it's music. Like discovering Lush in a field twenty-five years ago, sometimes you accidentally light upon something that you love and it stays with you.

CHAPTER 10

• • •

I should tell you about the fire.

But first, I want to tell you about when my mother stopped drinking, because that's what happened right before the fire, the first time I'd ever known her to actively try to be sober. It's important that she tried for lots of reasons, one of them being that it also led her to make her best decision for me with clarity, the decision to get me the abortion. If she hadn't quit drinking, and if our lives hadn't been such an insane, rocky mess at the time that I got pregnant, it's possible that I wouldn't have called her or, if I had, it would have been a mess. But it wasn't a mess. I've already told you. The abortion was the best thing that ever happened to me, because my mother walked me into it with clarity and a full heart. A sober mother making a sober decision.

And I have to believe now, thinking about it, that the abortion happened only because of the way everything directly before it collapsed. I could have gotten pregnant under many circumstances. But for the abortion to happen, everything had to have fallen apart.

My mother had veered increasingly out of control in the

months since her and my father had separated, though she managed to hold down her job. She drank almost daily, now that my father wasn't there to watch over her, and we, her kids, were no deterrent despite our constant arguments with her about it. She drove drunk a lot, something which pained all of us. Sometimes, if she didn't appear for dinner (meaning there was no dinner), we would just call down the street to the bar and ask for her. But more often than not, we didn't bother.

I don't remember much of what it was she was doing at that point, beyond working in an office somewhere. Since I'd been in about fifth grade or so, my mother had usually worked, mostly part time but sometimes full time. There was a sense, though I never confirmed it, that she would get a job, almost always in an office, as a secretary (what we would definitely now call an "assistant"), become well loved and highly valued, and then, one day, the job would sort of dissipate.

"I quit. They didn't pay me enough for the shit I put up with," she would say, and inevitably, I'm sure, that was true. Now, however, I suspect that my mother would make a work friend and after a short amount of time she'd reveal her addiction. Or at least the fact that she was often a very sloppy drunk. Because that always happened: my mother's new jobs usually brought about some new friendship with a single or divorced woman, they went out to "dinner" a bunch of times and then sometimes came to our house to drink and talk. Sometimes these other women friends were just as drunk as she was—drunkenness is normal enough on occasion, and at first I think it probably seemed to the friends to be nothing out of the ordinary. But my mother had a way of eventually letting her guard down, and it never worked out for her.

I think there was always a sense of endings on the way. The story of my mother's adult life, I see now, outside her family, was one of fast friendships that ended as soon as she drank with them enough times. I get it: it's hard to be around a drunk.

Anyway, my mother, my two brothers, and I became ships passing in the night, nobody looking anybody else too closely in the eyes, which I suppose was for the best. I wanted no scrutiny on myself, as I rolled joints in bathrooms and rolled my eyes at teachers who told me I could do better.

When I did go to school, I mostly skipped classes and hung out with Emily and Ellen and Vanessa, and I tried not to think too much. But the outside world barged in a lot in those days. In April of 1994, Kurt Cobain died (in addition to Richard Nixon); and on June 12 of that year, just three days before my birthday, Nicole Brown Simpson was murdered. June 17 was the O. J. Simpson Bronco chase. All of this, somehow, made sense to me, if I don't sound too ridiculous saying so. I felt myself surging toward adulthood: I would graduate from high school the following year, my parents were getting divorced, and the rest of the world was falling apart around me. In September of that year, just after I'd returned to school to begin what I hoped would be my final year of high school, USAir Flight 427 crashed just outside the airport in Pittsburgh as it was landing. Everyone on board died. Four of the people who died were from my hometown, and some of my fellow students lost their fathers.

I didn't make any of this about me; I didn't need to. My own life was sort of a mess too, and so I simply took it all in and moved forward. But the pall cast over the town where I lived and the people I was surrounded by was huge and black.

These are the only world events I remember from that year. What else was going on I cannot say, and I've never liked tying things together in neat little packages, relating unrelated events to one another in order to create symmetry, even if that symmetry is misery. But this feeling, that everything around me was suffocation, was palpable. Did my depression and anxiety go unnoticed? No: it was simply that everyone else was depressed and anxious too, in that time and in that place.

At some point that fall, my relationship with my first real boyfriend, Nick, began to end. Like most things, it was gradual until it was bluntly over. I had my gripes with him: he wouldn't go to my junior prom with me; he was "over" high school. I went with someone else, who I secretly also wanted to date. My feelings about relationships were fairly fluid. I wanted more boyfriends than one sometimes, and that seemed fine with me.

My mother and I began to argue about that, too. She could see clearly when I was fucking around, and even though she didn't really know much about it, one or two times she overstepped her boundaries—something she excelled at, especially drunk—and called Nick herself. Listening to her slur her words on the phone with my teenage boyfriend was more than I could bear but nothing I could stop. He humored her; he listened. I wanted to scratch out my own eyes as she complained bitterly about me to him.

Nick and I fought but remained close as the fall fell into winter: he was the only person I'd really been honest with about my mother, and that tie was hard to break. Once the floodgate of my honesty had opened, it couldn't be closed again. I started, quietly and slowly, to hand out bits of information to other people. And I became friends with Nick's friends, some of whom could relate to my home life.

I want to say exactly how all this unfolded, but I'm not sure. In January of 1995, just after Christmas, something terrible happened, which I ignored. I came home one afternoon to my mother locked in the bathroom. I couldn't tell what was going on, but I feared it was something awful. I did not investigate, because I was selfish and I guess I didn't care exactly what happened to my mother just then. We'd barely spoken to each other in recent months, and she drank nearly every day.

The light person she could be disappeared and was replaced almost completely by the dark one. The depressed mother I avoided at all costs. I left the house not knowing what my mother was doing locked in the bathroom, and I didn't come back until the next day.

By then, it was obvious: my mother had, drunk or sober, cut her wrists in the bathtub. Her friend from up the street who had been a nurse in a previous iteration but was now mostly a drinking buddy to my mom had been summoned. There were conversations I had with her, whispered. Should my father be called? Of course. My grandparents? Yes.

I don't remember those few days very well. I know that my mother did thankfully end up in a hospital, and I wasn't able to visit her for well over a week. I'm not sure how much time passed. I know that when I did visit her, my friend Patrick, who I'd met through Nick, took me there. He was kinder and quieter and more caring than Nick. He understood without me telling him much of what was happening. I didn't need to explain: he was bent toward sadness too, like me.

In that hospital, I found a small and changed woman. The

anger flowed out and was replaced by a need, a desperate need, to save. I was, as I'd been in third grade, the adult once again. My own problems ceased to exist; the teenage cares died away. I was sober, and so was she.

I worried, as I talked to her, to hear that her doctors would not really discuss what was going on with me directly. I worried, as I heard her say, "I'm depressed about your father," when I knew at a cellular level that she was an alcoholic. She said the depression caused the drinking.

"Of course I have to stop drinking, but that's not my real problem," she said. She looked so small as she lied to me. My mother was much shorter than me. I was five foot five; she barely grazed past five feet. She weighed one hundred pounds at most. Her wrists were wrapped up; she'd have those scars for the rest of her life.

"I didn't mean it," she told me there.

"I know," I said.

"I love you," she said.

"I love you, too," I said.

At home, in the meantime, my grandparents Peg and Stanley presided over their three grandchildren. My grand-father's advancing Alzheimer's meant that he was increasingly irritated by being away from home and paced back and forth constantly.

"She's smoking in the bathtub," I heard my grandma Peg say of me once, as I lay in the bathtub smoking.

My father, to the extent that I remember him then (I suppose I have a way of forgetting the men, with time), was panicked and constantly asking my brothers and me to live with him. We all, to our eternal detriment, declined. My father was a straight arrow: he was strict, not always easy to talk to, all business. He was simple and didn't drink much. I can recall seeing him drunk on only a number—a very small number—of occasions in my entire life, and even then he hadn't been wasted.

Why do children of alcoholics cling to the worse parent, the alcoholic? Well, I see even now in my relationship with Zelda that I am the "less fun" parent and that, in a standoff she would, certainly as a teen, choose her father over me. I am the rule keeper, the boss. That was my father. So maybe it was me staying to protect my alcoholic mother, or maybe I simply wanted to stay with her because she was easier.

Why did my mother do what she did? I suspect that she wanted to start fresh but didn't know how. I have suspected that maybe she realized too late that my father leaving wouldn't actually solve all her problems, as she had predicted many times. In this one case, however, I do not have any real theories or answers: I only know that this happened, and that it was gutting to everyone.

But it did reset us, sort of.

I began to take up childish pursuits that as a teenager I had abandoned. I started coloring and carrying an Elmo doll around with me. I clung to my friends, waiting for my mother to come back. I don't know how long she was gone, I guess close to a month, because it was nearly February by then. My grandparents were going out of their minds and had packed up and gone home. My brothers had somewhat grudgingly stayed with my dad for a bit, and I went not far up the street to Emily's house.

And that was how Wacky Wednesday started in earnest. Because suddenly, I was staying with Emily. We'd spent most of our childhoods alternating homes but now, really, I was there every minute of every day. Her mother packed me lunches and made sure I went to school. It lasted only a week or two before my mother came home.

I was happy to have her back, though I don't remember it very well. Everything seemed sort of tenuous. My grandparents reappeared and stayed again. My brothers returned, and we re-formed, silent, awkward glances and knowing stares.

My mother seemed better, but nothing felt permanent anymore. Would it hold?

And she had stopped drinking. She was on antidepressants and sleeping pills to counteract the antidepressants. I tried to go to school more, to pay attention and apply myself. I thought about taking the SAT, which I had never done before and was late on.

I think now that my mother's breakdown and attempt to harm herself physically was easily glossed over in some respect because it was followed so quickly by a long (relatively speaking) period where she reset and recharged. She seemed fragile, yes, but not weak. She seemed reinvigorated and more like the person we had known early in childhood. She was in therapy and AA. I want to believe that that was why I didn't focus for too long on what had come before: because she seemed so much better, truly, and because I desperately wanted her to be.

My grandparents shuffled back home at some point; my mother did seem stable and quite content, happier, to me, maybe than she had seemed in years.

But still, it was not much of a surprise to me when I came

home from school one snowy afternoon, the first Friday of February, packed into a Jeep with a bunch of friends to drop me off, to fire trucks parked in my giant front yard.

I jumped out of the car, dropped my books in the snow, and ran toward the house.

"You can't go in there," a fireman said, stopping me.

"Where is my mother?"

He said that she and my brother John had just left with a friend.

"She refused to go in an ambulance," he said, "though she was suffering from smoke inhalation."

"What about the cats?" I asked dumbly. We had two of them; they were always needing me to clean their litter boxes and feed them, and they'd become an enormous pain in my ass as my mother failed to care for them.

"We didn't find any cats," he said as he started to walk away. "You can't go in there."

I looked at the house, which was brick and no longer had a roof or half its windows. Police tape covered the doors.

I walked up the street, coatless—I never wore a fucking coat anywhere—to the neighbor's house. My mother and brother were there. I called Emily, then walked up to her house.

So it was that I stayed, again, with Emily. My mother and my brothers were moving an hour away to live with my grandparents while the house was sorted out. We didn't know if it could be repaired. Everything that I owned was presumably gone. I thought mostly about my pillow, a feather one that I had had since I was in a crib. I thought about my Lush records and my books. I knew none of it mattered.

I couldn't move in with my father; he lived too far away for me to finish at my school, of which I had just four months remaining. I wasn't technically allowed to live outside the school district, so we arranged, through Emily's mother, who told me I could live with them until June, something that was indescribably generous and still shocks me in how much it meant to me.

I returned to my house the next day. I pulled away the police tape from the back door and walked inside. Though it was very newly deserted, it felt as though it had been frozen in time. Snow had started to drift into the windows.

In the kitchen, I found the first cat, sitting under the kitchen table, meowing. I don't remember what friend of mine I had brought with me, but I took the cat out to him or her and then went back inside. It might have been one of my brothers who came with me. I remember only how fucking cold it was and how dark it seemed inside the house, where there was no longer any electricity.

I walked back through the kitchen and down the hall to my bedroom. My records, which had been on a shelf on the wall shared with my mother's room, where the fire had started, were melted down the wall. I took three books, all of which were covered in thick black soot. Anything I carried away from that house that day smelled of the fire forever. It's a smell I cannot forget.

I looked into my mother's room. The firemen had said it was an electrical fire, but I wondered if my mother, who had been asleep in bed when it started, had fallen asleep smoking. I couldn't be sure, though I worried that that was what had happened. Somehow, though it didn't matter, the thought of her having been the cause gnawed at me deeply.

My brother John, who had skipped school that day to play his guitar in the basement, told me only that she had run out screaming, the house filled with smoke, summoning him from the basement.

I found the other cat as I came back into the kitchen. I stood there, calling her name. She'd been through a lot. She was hiding in the basement, and just as I was about to give her up for dead or departed, she ran up the stairs. I had a carrier I'd brought from the neighbor, and I forced her into it. We left the house, I thought maybe for the last time. I didn't know that I would be back with my father very soon, inside the house, a dumpster in the driveway, throwing shit away and making lists for the insurance claims. I thought it was over at the time. That you could just go, "Well, fuck it, this one burned down."

But eventually, we did go back, and some things were salvaged from the house. From a chest in which my mother had kept treasures we pulled three photo albums of mostly our early childhoods and a box of random snapshots from later. I have those here, now. My mother's baby book came out of the fire somehow, though I never saw it until after she died. I know that it was in the house from the fire only because the edges of the white book are covered in that thick soot that smells like that day. But most of my own stuff was simply gone and truly forgotten. I don't know what I'm missing beyond simply almost everything. A few of my diaries from childhood, which had been boxed up in the basement, made it out. It didn't matter so much: for now, we were all still alive.

A year ago, I found something that I had never seen before while searching for local newspaper articles using my old address for an unrelated writing project. I found a small notice of the fire. It was very police blotter–style, straightforward, just a few words: fire in master bedroom, electrical.

Female in house refused medical care for smoke inhalation."
Got it. And though I'd carried with me for twenty years the
suspicion that my mother had actually started the fire by
smoking a cigarette and falling asleep in bed, I found that
same day another item in my Google search. In 1981, four
years before we bought the house and moved in, another fire:
"Master bedroom, electrical; no injuries." So there it was.
After years of wondering, a revelation. Maybe it was just an
accident after all.

My father lived only twenty minutes away but I didn't
drive. My mother and my brothers would be, in two days'
time, an hour's drive away. I owned nothing and had no one.
I was alone.

Less than a month and a half later, I was pregnant and
called my mother, who might as well have lived in Alaska and
was just two months' sober, to tell her.

CHAPTER 11

◆ ◆ ◆

Just six to eight weeks after the fire, while living at Emily's house with my mother and brothers an hour away and my father out of the loop on my personal life, my mother took me to get the abortion.

And then I graduated from high school—barely, but I did it, in June of 1995, just five days before my eighteenth birthday. My whole family was there, and from that day is the one of the only photos I have of my mother and me together, other than a few family portraits taken by a professional photographer when I was very young. It is a haunting photo, mostly because it's actually a photo of me and my grandmother and my great-aunt. We're smiling at the camera, and in the background, slightly out of focus and off to the side, wearing sunglasses and holding my graduation program, is my mom. She's looking away from us, at something else, just accidentally in the photo. She looks healthy and happy.

But before I graduated, there was one more fire.

And though I didn't start it, I took the blame.

After school on a Friday in late May, probably two weeks before I was scheduled to graduate, I had another one of my many detentions. Once detention concluded, I headed with a girl I knew fairly well but wasn't that close with to the bathroom by the cafeteria where we smoked in the handi-capped stall. We could easily pack half a dozen girls into that stall, smoking cigs and talking shit. We were in there, Chris and I, and eventually we were joined by another girl.

At some point, there in that stall, with cigarettes, a lighter, and a large can of aerosol hairspray, someone—not me, I can tell you that, though I'll never admit even now, who started it—lit the paper towel dispenser on fire. It seemed sort of funny at first. I don't think those bathrooms even had smoke detectors then, and anyway the fire was very small.

For a minute. But then it got larger. Everyone was laughing hysterically, then suddenly became nervous. This fire, which had one minute earlier seemed so destined to simply peter out, had actually grown.

We left the bathroom, and on our way out, a janitor saw us leaving. He must have gone into the bathroom and put out the fire. I left school that day in fear but also convinced that somehow it was no big deal.

But on Monday morning I was pulled from my first class, taken into the principal's office, and asked to explain what had happened. I refused. I left the office, and on my way out I saw the other two girls sitting there, waiting to be called in.

I don't remember all the details, but I do remember that, through conversations with the girls there, I realized both were afraid of their fathers. Afraid of them physically. They were crying, telling me that their parents simply couldn't hear about this. I remember one of them saying, "He'll send me away."

The situation hadn't seemed that serious to me, but when

I was called back to the principal's office, there was a man there who they said was the fire warden. The principal told me that I needed to admit and explain myself or else I would not graduate. I would be charged with a crime. I had no idea if any of it was true, and I said several times, "There's no way anyone can prove that I was even there."

"But we know that you were there," he said. I hated him so much.

"I want to call my mother," I said. She was too far away to come in on such short notice, so before I explained anything, I said that I was going to call her.

They took me to another office with a phone and left me alone.

I called my mother.

I explained my situation. I told her that I wanted to admit that I had done it, so that the other two girls wouldn't get in trouble. If I said it was me, that it was an accident, that I'd gotten scared and run away, I thought I could avoid being expelled two weeks before graduation and I could keep anyone else from getting in trouble.

My mother told me she would talk to the principal herself.

"Don't say shit to them," she said before hanging up.

That was the end of it. I was suspended for the last two weeks of graduation activities, though I went to classes. Most of the time I was in the library, alone, while the rest of my class went to water parks and practiced, getting ready for the graduation ceremony. Being there alone in the library, reading quietly, I felt, was a fitting end to my high school career. I'd felt solitary among hundreds of kids for a pretty long time and was happy to end this way.

I'd spent the last few weeks of my high school career

staying with my father, after Emily's mom had, unsurprisingly, found two teenagers on the cusp of adulthood to be a bit much for her to handle. This was a very good thing on so many levels: I went to school each day; my father drove me there and dropped me off, making sure I was in attendance. I left each afternoon on time; he picked me up from Emily's house or a friend drove me back to his place in the evening. I guess I ended my high school career on the highest possible note, given everything that had happened.

But I had no plans for the future.

I felt compelled to move back in with my mother, though, and so I did, just weeks after graduation. I packed up my next to nothing, and I went an hour away to live with her in the new house she had rented. It was a huge, beautiful old Victorian that had been converted into apartments, but it had no other tenants, so the house felt like it was ours.

I moved there at the same time my mother did, when she moved out of my grandparents' house, where her and my brothers had been staying since the fire. This was a time of great optimism for me, and, I think, for all of us. My mother seemed very healthy. She still wasn't drinking, and she threw herself into decorating and organizing a new home for all of us.

My bedroom in that apartment, though I lived there less than a year, is one that I still dream of. It was completely paneled in old cherry boards, and when the door was closed, you couldn't even really see that there was a door there. The room's two casement windows were nearly floor to ceiling. The floors were cherry, and one wall was covered in built-in bookshelves. This room seemed meant for me; it was literally a cozy cave of a room where I could hide and read all day. I loved it and felt very happy to be there.

I enrolled at a nearby college and tried not to think too much about the future. I felt unsure and weak, as though I'd just gotten over a new sickness and was still wobbly, a just-born giraffe trying to walk. I wanted to be happy, to feel as though I could scream from the rooftop, but really, everything seemed so tenuous.

The fact that my mother quit drinking, even for less than one year, was magical in some ways. It is those months that I now think back on when I want to think of good times with my mother, because in that small space, we made up for some lost time. I had a new and growing circle of friends and a very active social life suddenly and I was going to school, but my mother and I spent a lot of time together.

She couldn't drive anymore; she'd lost her license for, I'm not sure, possibly forever—I never really knew her to drive again in her life—so I'd shuffle her back and forth to work and we'd walk around the neighborhood we lived in.

We shopped and decorated the house; we cooked and cleaned together. We bought books and made sure my brothers went to school. We giggled at soap operas in the afternoon, and we spent hours watching the O. J. Simpson trial. We watched CNN constantly. My mother was a great lover of the Clintons, and all my grandparents were those ardent, union-loving kind of Catholics who yelled at the TV about Republicans. My grandfather's Alzheimer's was advancing, and my mother and I spent a lot of time in that period with him and my grandmother. Though my grandmother's cutting remarks didn't recede completely, my mother seemed suddenly more confident and able to let them slide off her back than she had been in the past. Their relationship seemed stronger, too.

My mother's sobriety did not hold. This was not surprising, though I don't think it was a judgment on her to say I
wasn't surprised. My understanding of alcoholism, even then,
meant that expectations—any, even low ones—should basically not exist. I wanted her to be healthy and sober, but I
couldn't control that, and I knew it.

I'd like to say that I had learned something from the
previous years, that I called up friends or family and asked
them to help us, but I didn't. I receded into my old patterns.
I withdrew into a world where I partied with new friends I'd
made. I tried to get along, I started skipping classes immediately, and, most important, I didn't tell anyone who could
have offered help what was going on.

Here's the part where I begin to talk about guilt and how
I blame myself for failing my mother. I've thought this clus-
terfuck through so many times I get lost in the pathways of
who should have been responsible for whom, and I know that
there is no way to make full sense of it.

But by then, the disappointment of seeing my mother,
who had clocked less than a year of sobriety and who in that
time had truly seemed to be the person I'd always known she
was, drinking again was not unexpected. I don't know why: I
need to give her credit for those months of effort. I did give
her credit, even then. I'm sure, I know now, that they were a
devoted effort, and the time we spent together, just doing
normal things—like shopping, cooking, cleaning the house,
watching movies— is time I am happy to have banked into my
memory.

But still, when she started drinking again, everything was
worse than it had been before. She moved quickly; her addiction became aggressive and relentless. She stopped caring

what I thought, and we fought bitterly and constantly. I told her I hated her. I told my father I hated him too, for good measure. I hated everyone and everything. I shaved my head and got tattoos I didn't want or need. I started drinking again myself: I'd been sober for much of her sobriety, committed, I think, even if sort of unknowingly, to making a go at something different. And when she failed, I failed with her.

But it couldn't hold. My life was too new.

My brother Daniel left first. He disappeared basically overnight. I wasn't there when it happened, was staying in a dorm room with a friend. I came home on a Saturday morning, and my brother John told me: he'd packed up a garbage bag of clothes after some rancid blowout fight with my mother, who had been drunk. He'd called my dad to pick him up, and he was gone.

As soon as he left, he flourished with my father while the rest of us floundered. He went to school, he had a more normal life of a sixteen-year-old kid.

I sputtered and didn't know where to turn or what to do. I dated boys who were just as fucked up as I was, who understood nothing or everything, depending on what I told them. There were lots of nights where I rushed out of the house and didn't come back for days. There were nights of arguments. I didn't hold back when she was drunk; I told her she needed to stop even though I knew my words might as well have gone unsaid.

When I'd talked to my mother about her drinking as a child, I'd been subtler, more pleading on her behalf. Now, as a young adult, I was blunter. I screamed and begged and sometimes wanted to shake her, to hit her.

Instead, I left. I left not knowing what to do or where to

go except that I had friends who would take me in for a while. I left without taking anything, my mother screaming behind me, "You'll be back!" I left on foot.

I had no job or car or money. Everything I'd had was hers, and I was determined that I was never coming back, I'd never live with her again. I was eighteen years old. I'd dropped out of school after two semesters and hadn't even attended any classes of the second.

"You don't know what it is to be on your own, to take care of yourself," she said to me that day, later on the phone, when I'd called her back simply because I wasn't done screaming yet.

"I'm going to find out," I said.

CHAPTER 12

. . .

A nd I did find out. It took me more than a year to go back
to school. A year to get a job, an apartment of my own,
a boyfriend who was nice and supportive. I got a dog and
eventually a cat. I bought a car, and I figured out how to do
my taxes and how to apply for financial aid and loans.

My mother was very bad with money. As a growing adolescent, I made a point never to open the hallway closet where
we stored random papers, old photo albums, report cards, and
school projects. Though I've always loved paper, I grew to
hate the sight of mail and bills. My mother hid things like
bills. My father basically handled the finances as my mother's
problems grew. But, like a child hiding a bad grade, my mother
hid report cards and bills as if hiding them would make them
disappear. Knowing, as I grew into an adult, that that is not
what happens—another bill simply comes until there are
worse consequences, late fees, a shut-off phone—I find it hard
to fathom what she thought she was accomplishing.

"Out of sight, out of mind" seemed to be her ruling philosophy.

And once my parents were divorced, these matters

became more pressing, of course. With just one adult to ensure the rent was paid and with less income than we'd formerly had, hidden bills did quickly blossom into occasionally picking up the landline to silence: no dial tone; the phone has been shut off. Then we'd go to my mother, she'd pay the bill, and they'd turn service back on. If she'd had the money all along, I wondered, why the aversion to paying the bills in the first place?

I learned later that this is very common behavior for alcoholics, that they avoid doing things that cost almost nothing, like renewing their driver's license, out of a simple inability to deal with everyday things.

After my parents divorced we moved in with my mother; my father had decided to live in the same house we'd grown up in, the one that had burned down. It had taken months to repair and rebuild it, but he had persisted in doing so. He loved that house and wasn't ready to leave it. He stayed there until well after I was married, and eventually, the old bad memories were indeed replaced with new ones. In fact, the rebuilding, the repainting, all that effort made it so that very quickly after the fire, as soon as he'd moved back in, I was able to walk through the house almost as if it hadn't happened. When I'd heard he was going to live there, I'd felt conflicted: so many bad things had happened there in that last year. Would I feel horrible any time I was inside? But I found that it soothed me to be inside of it. To go into the room that had been my bedroom, my sanctuary as a child, and see its walls, now painted white and clean, still standing.

In order to stay living there, of course, my father had paid my mother for half the house in their separation. I don't know how much money it was, but it was a lump sum of cash, and whatever that amount was, at the time it had seemed vast. It was enough that my mother could have made a fresh, independent financial start for herself. My grandparents, her parents, were very good with money and were easy in their retirement. I remember that they offered to help her manage her newly acquired money. She didn't refuse them, but she also never took them up on the offer.

In less than a year, my mother simply spent through the money and ended up with nothing to show for it. She bought clothing and jewelry and gifts for us, paid cash for things, and began racking up a lot of credit card debt. I watched as a bystander as this happened and had her cosign credit applications for myself.

I'd taken a personal finance class in high school, so I knew that she was proceeding unwisely. She could have bought a house, but she rented. She could have invested a part of her lump of cash, but she kept it in her checking account. She didn't even get interest on what was not a tiny amount of money. But only in hindsight did I understand how terrifically she mismanaged her money.

By the time I moved from her apartment, the money was mostly gone. Her job, which paid very little, was not enough to offset her debts, and she was on shaky ground, like previous jobs, with them anyway. I left fearing for how she would manage but had to strike out on my own. I felt exhausted before I'd even begun, but a sense of great relief replaced my worries very quickly as my daily life vastly improved once removed from my mother, even though I was only a mile away. I worried about her but pushed it back further and further into my mind as I realized that my life and her life were actually distinct lives, not one jumbled messy one.

I was determined to learn from her mistakes but bumped along the way myself. I made my rules then: since I had to pay for everything on my own, for school and life, I wouldn't drink. I couldn't fuck up school again; I couldn't afford to. I never wanted to go back to my mother, who would soon be shuttling through jobs and boyfriends quickly.

I saw my mother only on holidays, and even that was like stabbing myself in the face with a butter knife. After two years away from her, I allowed that she seemed to have set her own path. By then, my brother John had also moved back in with my father to finish high school and have a chance at something resembling a normal ending to his childhood. In order to graduate from high school, every single one of us had to leave our mother for our father, even if only temporarily.

She was mean and meek at the same time. Her defense mechanism seemed to increasingly be retreating into childlike simplicity and defeat. She was who she was, she said. "I'm a drunk," she said to me on the phone once. "Are you happy?"

I wasn't, not exactly. In fact, though I cooked and cleaned and had the beginnings of a normal, domestic life on top of being a somewhat normal college student, happiness was hard to come by.

I dedicated myself to doing well in school, to learning, not really for a job but just to have something pure and clean to apply myself to. I learned, even in my job waiting tables, that work was the thing that could wash away my feelings of anxiety and fear and sadness. I couldn't get rid of those feelings, not while my mother was alive and drinking fifteen minutes away from my own apartment, but I could sidestep the feelings temporarily. I could work.

I worked. I worked so much. I went to school full time,

part time in the summers, trying to make up for those first two horrific semesters. I worked after school every day and usually full days on the weekends, volunteering to wash dishes and bus tables on days when I wasn't scheduled to wait tables. I found that, by having little spare time to think, I could in fact move on in a way. I couldn't escape; I didn't want to escape. But I could move forward myself.

I was, unlike my mother, at the beginning of my life. And she resented me for that. In her worst moments, she resented me, I see now, for having that abortion, for choosing not to have a child, for deciding not to let life simply happen to me. My mother, though she had made her choices and built an incredibly beautiful family despite her addiction, felt, as she veered toward the end of her life, like a victim of circumstances. That made me saddest of all. But I also knew it was generational: most of the women her age I knew, friends' mothers, had also had similarly limited options despite being raised in relative privilege. Her life could have been different if she'd wanted it to be. She'd only ever begun to express dissatisfaction with how it was recently, and I had trouble seeing what it had to do with my own different choices. In hindsight too, I see that a great part of the reason I waited to have Zelda so long was the fact that I wanted a career, and it took so long to find one, to build it and work on it, that I simply couldn't find space for a child for a very long time.

Early on, there were times when I still called her and said things like, "You're still so young! You should go back to school, you should go to rehab, you could do anything that you want! Anything!" I knew that her parents had money and still thought of her as a child in lots of ways. They'd help her; they'd pay anything to see her succeed. But what my mother needed most wasn't money, and if there was anyone on the planet who could have talked her into rehab, well, that person wasn't me. It wasn't any of my brothers. It wasn't my father.

I don't hold my mother's financial failures against her. Unlike me, now learning to live life on my own with no real safety net to buffer me from life's realities, my mother had never lived on her own. She'd gone straight from the safety of her parents to that of my father, who I think had been austerely committed to financial solvency by nature. Women of her generation were often not expected to worry about money, I reasoned. So, when she found herself divorced and unemployed in a new apartment with three kids, child support, and a lump of money in her early forties, she was completely unprepared for managing on her own. And the fact that people offered to help, I'm sure, made her bristle: in the early days of her sobriety, she took the concept of independence very much to heart. She didn't want to run to her parents for advice; she was a grown woman, she would say. I understood that: independence is hard to acquire when you're not used to it, and once you taste it, it's easy to guard it misguidedly, when asking for a little bit of help would be smarter.

But she also failed to think of her children the way that I think I myself would. She failed to plan for us, so when my tuition bill for my second semester came due and we didn't quite have the money to cover it, I had to call my father. And, of course, she'd failed to help me apply for financial aid, aid that I was surely able to qualify for. My mother was never good at planning that way.

So I had to learn all on my own the process of paying my bills and taxes and learning how to get financial aid so that I'd be able to go to school. I knew, in the back of my mind, that if I hit a bad spot, my father would help me in any way that he could, but like my mother, I became stubborn to the concept of asking for help. Unlike her, after a while, I managed pretty well on my own.

I don't give up on people, and I didn't consciously give up on my mother. But by the time I was nearing five years out of high school, around the year 2000, I would say, the distance between my mother and I emotionally was widening to a gulf. She was fading, somehow, in my mind. When I visited her, I always found something to be depressed about, to focus on. The fact that she was now so clearly financially unstable, that she couldn't hold a job, saddened me. My brothers and I had all managed to pull through our childhoods and come out as, to one degree or another, somewhat sane adults. How they did so I can't say, but, how I did it was largely by pulling away from my mother almost completely.

And I'd pulled away from my father, too. There were times in those years where I simply didn't talk to anyone in my family, not because I was angry, but because it just didn't make sense. I was surviving.

I've found that in order to survive an alcoholic parent, sometimes it's best to narrow your interests down to the finest point: yourself. Focusing on me had never been easy. It still isn't; I excel at worrying about others. But for a solid five years, the ones that mattered very, very much and made me an adult, I aggressively guarded myself. I lost track of old friends and ignored the calls of family.

I'm not proud of myself in those years, when I think back on it now, and I realize that I have described it in the best possible light up to this point. In reality, I didn't visit my dying

grandfather nearly enough, or my healthy but aging grandmothers. These visits became painful reminders of my mother,
who I could not help. They constantly asked about her. "She's
good," I'd say, trying not to laugh or holding back tears. How
many times have I lied and told people, "She's pretty good"?
Too many to count. I'd decided, so many times, that I'd never
mention her alcoholism again to her. But then, six months or
a year would pass, and I'd end up researching rehab facilities
and calling her yet again.

It's important for me to say that in these years, from the
time I graduated from high school on, we never—no one
ever—managed a true intervention with my mother, of the
kind where you meet up in person and confront the person in
order to get them to rehab. Though I've participated in several of these, they've all happened in the years since my
mother died. Had I known then what I know now about
interventions—that they very often work—I would have
pushed harder for one for her, rather than pushing directly at
her on my own. Had I known that instead of years of nagging,
a simple, emotional, and possibly embarrassing group conversation might have flipped a switch inside her, I would have
pulled that together.

But I didn't know that. I felt scared of taking such a step,
and I worried about embarrassing her. I'm sure it's no accident
that one thing an alcoholic doesn't want—group attacks and
the airing of laundry—is often what works, but it's sad because
the people who love that person most *also* avoid the same
types of situations because of years of conditioning. I have
avoided confrontations of this kind all my life, for no reason.
I don't fear embarrassment or arguments or even healing of

any type. It was simply a habit born of years of anxiety, to avoid anything I would generically label as confrontation. Until Josh came along, I fought against confrontation at all cost.

Confrontation comes in many forms: I have a lifelong habit of not liking to or being able to finish things, thanks to my hatred, my phobia of confrontation. I first noticed it with school. I wasn't bad at school—in fact, I was good at school—but in college I would put off doing papers and work until just hours before their due date, and then have to rush through to make it on time. I knew this was normal college kid stuff, but I felt so much attendant guilt that I began to wonder where it came from and started to note in my diary other ways in which I avoided finishing things and confrontations: they're twins.

I struggled to finish college and beat out my worst tendencies to not finish things. Even as a college senior, after years of working full time and taking summer classes to make up for lost time, I occasionally just collapsed in on myself and blew a class at the end of the semester, getting an F where I'd been getting an A just weeks earlier, not even bothering to email the professor to try to negotiate for an extension or some special consideration. I was a terrible advocate for myself but was slowly learning not to avoid hard conversations if they were in my interest.

I found that it was okay to admit this flaw to other people, that even employers would sometimes "get it." "I have a hard time finishing things," I'd say. I worked on the weekends for years as a caterer, mostly working at weddings. These kinds of jobs suited me because they paid well—it was about the most money I could make without an education—and they were finite: we rolled in with a job to do and rolled back out eight or nine hours later. We put up a tent in a field or a backyard, built a little kitchen out back, served 150 people their dinners and their cake and coffee, cleaned everything up, threw it into a truck, and zapped ourselves back out of it. Hard labor, the kind with a definite end point, didn't trouble me.

What continued to rankle me, for years, was finishing *Middlemarch* or the dishes in my kitchen sink. For a decade I watched as I washed every dish in the sink before stopping, nearly but not wholly done, a coffee mug or two left behind. Just yesterday I had to silently chide myself for almost leaving the silverware laying there in the bottom of the otherwise empty sink for literally no reason at all.

I wash the silverware. I finish the book. I make the phone calls I need to make. I renew my driver's license. I take the dog to the vet.

Becoming a moderately effective adult in spite of my mother, has, I see, been largely a matter of simply completing all the mundane little tasks of life, which she never could do. I shudder any time I think of an unpaid bill, remembering the way that sometimes I'd open a closet door at home and a pile of unopened mail would fall on my head from a high-above shelf. She tinkered on the brink of extinction constantly: the lights were never shut off, but she often couldn't handle basic tasks, even when she had ready money, paying up only when forced with immediate cancellation. Never impoverished, my mother insisted on pushing the boundaries of her wallet at every turn. Becoming an adult has meant pushing back against that same impulse toward self-destruction.

I persist; I check my credit score. I try to laugh at how silly all of it is and how easily it is, in theory, to not do as she did.

I graduated from college and "took a year off," by which I

mean I worked full time, managing one of the restaurants I had worked at through college and thinking about what I wanted to do next. I started a band with three other women as I eventually began applying to graduate schools. Though I applied to schools outside Pittsburgh and was accepted to two of them, I decided to stay there and to go to Carnegie Mellon for a year to study English literature. I wanted to go to graduate school mostly because I think I would have liked to stay in college longer. I wasn't ready to be finished. I felt at once both like a kid and an old lady. I was in some ways very mature—I took care of myself and my apartment and my pets and my taxes—but in others I was sort of underdeveloped. Graduate school seemed to me like a way to defer adulthood a little longer.

And the truth is, I still wanted to stay physically near my mother. This shamed me to think it, that I wanted to be vigilant, somehow, over a person I refused to see most of the time. Only as the years passed, as I learned that physical distance from my mother didn't matter so much, and as I learned to navigate my own life, did I realize that a near-constant state of panic about even minor woes—financial, emotional, whatever—wasn't normal.

Josh and I had started our lives together with relatively little in the way of money. Neither of us had savings or 401(k) accounts. But slowly we'd managed to begin saving; we'd bought a house; our credit scores were good. By the time Zelda was born, we had no debt other than my student loans, which, because I'd gone to graduate school and borrowed money for years, were significant. But we'd been slowly paying those down and were comfortable. It would be hard to overstate what that type of solvency—which isn't exactly wealth but is knowing that, even if a large bill comes up unexpectedly, you'll figure it out together—has meant to me. Slowly, we learned to be adults together. Slowly, we managed. And not having to worry, as I'd worried first with my mother, and then on my own, ceaselessly about such matters was very important to my overall peace of mind.

To be clear, it wasn't even so much a question of having enough money to cover things but more a question of how matters of money were confronted. Josh had no background of simply ignoring anything, let alone a pressing financial concern. I'd grown up differently, with a woman who often didn't confront these things as a matter of personal policy. Learning another way was hard for me but ultimately brought me to a place of greater security.

When Zelda was born, against some little voice inside of me that said, "Don't hide things," I opened a savings account for her, in her name, without telling Josh. I began to secretly funnel in small amounts of money. Ironically, when you consider my mother, I had become our family financial manager. I kept track of and paid the bills, I dealt with the tax preparers and the mortgage and the banks. When we bought our house, I managed much of the paperwork on my own. And so, when little gifts of cash came to me or to Zelda, when I got a freelance check for something I'd written, I would deposit parts of that into her account.

I don't know why I didn't immediately tell Josh about it. He certainly would have been in favor of saving for her, and it's not like he would ever take money meant for Zelda. But I quickly realized that it was an old habit, a part of me still unwilling to fully trust anyone with my security, and now Zelda's, that had led me to open the account without saying anything.

There wasn't a specific fear but a general sense that something might collapse, that the bottom might fall out, like our life was a cheap paper coffee cup. Two or so months after I opened the account, I casually mentioned it to Josh.

"I opened a savings account for Zelda, just in case, for education or I don't know what," I said.

"Good," he said.

What was so hard about that?

CHAPTER 13

· · ·

When my mother became a mother, she was new to adulthood. She'd never managed her own checking account. If she'd had a job, it had been for spending money. She'd been one of her parents' two children, had been given "the best of everything," as my grandmother liked to say. She'd gone to private Catholic school from kindergarten through college, and her parents bought all her expensive clothes and made sure she didn't want for anything. You could say she was spoiled, but as a mother now myself, I am averse to that word sometimes, being as I am so enthusiastically committed to my daughter's well-being.

But my mother never had a career. She'd taken another path, that of—for the most part—a full-time mother. I couldn't imagine being a mother at her age, barely out of high school. But she'd also had financial support from her family that I'd never had much of. She passed through her years of college debt-free, and I'd rejected, for most of my childhood and a large part of my early adulthood, the idea that I would ever even get married. I saw myself, partly because my mother encouraged me to do so, differently.

And from a very young age, I wanted to be a writer or a teacher. I liked school and learning even if I didn't always perform well as a student. I loved to read and write. I began keeping a daily diary when I was still in elementary school and have kept that habit ever since. My diaries are kept in plastic tubs in the garage now, but for years I moved them around in cardboard boxes, hiding them away from possible prying eyes, until finally, when we bought our house in Brooklyn, I shelved them in my office. "You can read these if I die," I said to Josh. There are hundreds of notebooks filled with my scrawl dating back to the 1990s.

And though I suppose I considered myself a narrator of myself for so long, I didn't ever think of writing about my own life seriously until I met Josh, who told me very early in our relationship that he thought it was great fodder for something: a novel, a memoir, a movie.

By the time Zelda was born, I had been writing professionally full time for seven years. I'd written about anything that struck my fancy, mostly the weird things I saw on the internet, or books, or video games. I kept little blogs where I wrote about pop culture or music. I wrote for tech blogs. But still, I'd never seriously considered writing about myself.

Writing that way is an intrusion first on yourself and your own privacy, and then, secondarily but often more problematically, on the other people in your life. But I avoided writing about myself mostly because I was a deeply guarded person. My mother was dead by then, and most of my friends knew my secret: my mother had been an alcoholic.

Sometimes, we avoid for good reason doing something that is very obvious and meaningful. Sometimes, it simply doesn't occur to us.

I've said before that giving birth to Zelda broke me open. It did so literally, the little cut on my belly that I tell Zelda about every night now before bed. That part is important to her: that physically, she was pulled from just beneath my belly button. But her birth broke me open to being able to make new and different friends, and it also opened me up to wanting to explore my experience as a mother in my writing.

I didn't start doing so consciously.

When Zelda was six months old, we got a nanny named Val. Her job was, at first, just two days a week, to care for baby Z with me in the house. They started to venture out into the summer sun very quickly, and I managed my tears at the separation.

I'd decided not to go back to the full-time job I'd had as an editor before she was born. "I think I'd like to try writing as a freelancer," I said to Josh one evening as we sat on the patio in our little backyard after Zelda went to sleep.

"I think that if you're ever going to do it, now is the time," he agreed.

Freelancing would allow me to be around Zelda, to be more flexible. I didn't want to be a full-time mother; I knew that. But I also knew, now that I'd formed a close bond with my daughter, that I didn't want to be away from her constantly, either.

I had financial concerns, of course. In the time Josh and I had been together I'd never not had a full-time salary. I did not make as much money as Josh did, but I also didn't make so much less that losing my salary would be meaningless. But Josh supported me, not by saying, "I will support you financially," but by saying, "I think you can do this well enough to make a lot of money." He believed in me, and that helped me believe in myself.

But when I finally arranged for and hired Val, and trained her to follow my rules about sleeping and eating, I found that for a few weeks, I was happy just to tinker around the house, to sleep, to read, and to catch up on previously missed doctor's appointments. I reorganized the kitchen and my office, cleaned out our bedroom closet, and realphabetized our books.

And slowly I thought, "I can make space for myself once again." I knew that the space I wanted now wasn't for personal leisure time. I'd never been good at relaxing or vacationing, and Josh was the same. For us, working was what made us good company for each other in our off hours, and now that Zelda was part of our family, I knew that working was what would make me complete.

I thought back to when my mother had gone back to work as her children went off to school, and I got it. I wondered if she'd wanted something more, to find a place where all her creative energies could be funneled. She didn't have a career, but she was a worker at heart. For me, the effort even devoted to waiting tables in college had been time I felt productive, and I see that it must have been meaningful for her, in her thirties, to go back to doing something outside of her home. I felt the same when Zelda was six months old, which was longer by half than I'd expected before she was born to be not working. I briefly thought, "Maybe I'll go up the street and apply for a job as a barista."

I wasn't sure; I felt at a crossroads. I had the time to myself to write. I had the means to live for a while without a consistent paycheck, and I was free to write absolutely anything that I wanted, to pitch pieces to whomever I chose.

One night, after Val had gone home and I'd put Zelda to bed, but before Josh had come home from work for the day, I sat down at my computer. I wanted to write something, but I didn't know what. I had barely kept up my diary in the preceding months, breaking years of habit. I'd written grocery lists and sleeping charts but almost nothing else in six months, an eternity to someone who normally takes notes on reading for fun.

I stared at the blank screen and exhaled.

And then, without any assignment or reason for doing so, I wrote an essay about my daughter. About how I'd lost time, months, to the weird space created by caring ceaselessly for a newborn baby. Without thinking about it, I sent it off to an editor I knew, who published it within days. I was walking my daughter up the street in a stroller on our way back from the post office when it was published online, and for a moment I stopped there on the sidewalk in shock.

I realized just then what I'd done—I'd written about myself and Zelda, and I hadn't at all considered what it would mean for us. But I felt great, like the spell of those six months had been broken, like I was active and in the world again. I felt a little nervous about being candid and open with an outside world, an incalculably vast world that encompasses possibly everyone. I'd spent so much of my life guarding my innermost thoughts and had suddenly broken that rule to muse aloud and publicly, to put my feelings out into the world. It felt good to do this. It felt raw and weird and exhilarating to write whatever I thought and not feel shame or confusion about how it would look. All of my mother's years of worries about appearances died right there.

I never considered before Zelda was born that I might

write about motherhood, about that experience with all its massive ups and downs. I didn't even consider it as I began doing it. I simply began, and rather than trying to find a voice to do it, I used the voice I already had. In those first essays I found a space to complain about the boring days, to focus on minute details of babyhood that I had observed and wondered at. And slowly I realized I wasn't writing about my daughter so much as I was writing about myself. And to my surprise, I was comfortable with it. I felt emboldened but also protected, in the way that saying something is bothering you aloud can often help to protect you, to make you feel immune to it. And I believe that this also gave me the ability to be a woman and a mother in a way that simply was never available to my mother. I claimed these identities simultaneously.

And I began to feel sad, occasionally, about the fact that my mother had never told me about what I increasingly felt must be true and what I endeavored to explore in my writing: that motherhood is not always easy, but more than that, it's not always fulfilling. It's really, really hard and sometimes disappointing.

She never told me if she felt conflicted about being a mother, the way that I now knew that I did. I felt torn in many directions by the simple fact of my daughter's existence. Because in the space of hours that I now began to make time for each day, five days a week to write, were hours lost that I could be spending with my daughter. And for me, motherhood meant feeling both that I desperately needed and wanted the space to be creative, to work, and to also swallow somewhat unhappily that I would sometimes rather give up and just spend my time with my daughter.

It's a paradox central to modern parenting: I wanted to be

with her all the time, and yet I didn't want to be with her all the time.

Over the course of months I began to accept my own ambivalence, to understand that this is actually how it works: that hours spent away from Zelda are required to make me a whole person, a dedicated and loving one, engaged with her in the time that I do spend with her. That if I spent twenty-four hours a day with her, I would actually be a lesser person. I would have little to offer her. And a necessary side effect of that, of course, is that sometimes I miss her. I never miss a school event, now that she's in school, or a special occasion. I handle a lot of the family holidays and am there every night to put her to bed. I have dinner with her every night. Working from home has been the best option for me, because I do want to be there with her every morning when she wakes up, to dress her and pack her lunch.

But I think that the ambiguity, the times when I miss her, are fuel for me to work harder. I often put Zelda to bed and work for another few hours at night simply to get more done so that I never have to work on weekends. I try not to look at my email or phone when I'm with her, to really be there.

There has been a sort of rolling debate in magazines and online over the past few years about what motherhood does to women's creativity, mostly writers', because they're the ones, after all, who write most often about the experience of motherhood.

I have had this debate myself, and often with Josh when I'm on a deadline and strapped for time. I have a hard stop each weekday at 5:15 p.m., when I need to go get Zelda. This is mostly a good thing, since it allows me to step away and get distance, literally, from my work. Then, at 8:30 p.m. or so, I'll go back to it fresher. But there's no question that the demands of motherhood force us to become adept planners and managers of our own time that, even still, many men do not succumb to when they become fathers.

Motherhood is not a job, exactly, but it's labor, and it's labor that doesn't respect our own sick days or the deadlines of our actual jobs. Many times I've been forced to simply give up working for days at a time because Zelda is home sick from school. I feel fortunate that I have the flexibility to do it, of course, but it sometimes creates overwhelming periods of stress where it simply feels as though I'm not doing a good job at anything. This is a normal working mother's experience, I know.

But for me, Zelda has prodded and added to my creativity, not stifled it. Not simply because I often write about her, though she is a great source of material. It's that my time has become more valuable, day to day, week to week, and inside of me it's created a rush to get to things before the hours run out. I have limited time to work each day, so I try to make the time count. That doesn't mean I don't occasionally blow half a morning dicking around on the internet. But it does mean that, more than at any other point in my life, I am making the most of my time, because it is so precious, and there is so little of it. I used to work sixty or seventy hours a week before I was a mother. Now, I work about forty-five or fifty. But in the three and a half years my daughter has been alive, I've written and published more than I had in all the previous seven I'd been working before she was born. She's made me more productive, and I think she's made my writing better and more honest.

Where before I used to think that all the stars needed to be aligned to force writing up and out of myself and onto a page, now, I have discovered, later in life than I would have liked, it can sometimes simply be forced by a strict stopping time every single day, out of me like vomit when I've got the flu.

I think too, more generally, that being a mother has made me so aware of my own mortality that I simply feel a rush to get to everything meaningful out of me that I can. I don't consciously think this way almost ever, but every day with a baby, and then a small child, feels incredibly vital. There are hundreds of moments each week that stop me in my tracks with their originality: I've never felt this or done this before. I've never heard a child describe the life cycle of a frog or known how their head feels when they have a cold. And that has made me observant of detail and pressed to document.

One of the things I took away from my conversations with my mother about kids and the fact that I decided not to have a child when I was still a teenager was that my mother didn't want me to not have the option to do it another way. She didn't want me to be a victim of circumstance, of an accident. She understood, whether any of her kids were "accidents" or not, what I couldn't understand then and what I really couldn't understand until I gave birth myself: there is nothing more irrevocable than a child. It is life-changing in all the good ways but also in plenty of unexpected and sometimes bad ways. My mother knew that if I had a child at eighteen, I would possibly never go to college or have the career that I wanted, and she helped me to reject that path for another one.

What is difficult, of course, is trying to fit these pieces of reality in with the facts of my own existence: Did my mother helping me to make my choices differently mean that she had some regrets about the way her own life had worked out? She always insisted we were the greatest thing to have ever happened to her, but as a teenager and a young adult, this prospect tortured me, that my mother might have some regret about having had us, that she might have harbored hopes for a different life for herself. I didn't want that to be true.

What I did not understand until I became a mother myself is that everyone has these doubts, as far as I can tell. I desperately wanted to have Zelda, to become a mother when I became one, and still there were days where I wondered if I'd made a mistake, if I wasn't "cut out" for parenthood, if I wouldn't rather be on a beach somewhere reading paperbacks for six days straight. Everyone occasionally wonders what the other path would look like. It's just a question of what you do with the path you're on.

CHAPTER 14

* * *

O nly once I was living alone, in my own apartment, going
  to college and working and taking care of myself, did I
get enough distance from the material reality of my family
that I could see the truth of what my mother's alcoholism had
done to us.

I was at an age when distancing oneself from parents in
order to forge an identity of one's own is very common and a
natural part of becoming an adult. But like every other
milestone in my life, the alcoholism confused and complicated. It fractured my relationships, not just with my
mother but with everyone. I became closer to my brothers but
still often felt distant from them. I held my father, who now
had a serious girlfriend, at an arm's length for years. We were
cordial, we spent holidays together, but so much had happened
that often it felt easiest to simply keep the talk on a surface
level. In fact, it felt nice to not have to talk about anything
tragic or serious sometimes, to keep the level of discourse
focused on something mundane.

I think my brothers fared better in this area with my dad
than I did, because they all had sports to some degree. They

could talk about Alabama college football or the Steelers or golf. I had no interest in sports and was desperately bad at feigning. Josh has always criticized my ability to make small talk with strangers, but I have found that this is a true characteristic of me even when I know people very well. I am capable of bullshitting if something worth discussing presents itself, but in the lack of that, I often find myself to be taciturn and silent enough to make those around me uncomfortable. I've worked hard on this, but it's still there.

And with my father, who is also bent toward silence, it meant that we didn't have much to talk about for a very long time. And honestly, that was okay: as I said, in order for me to become an adult, one who functioned and was in any way successful, I found that I had to collapse in on myself and be selfish for a very long time. And in those years, my family waited patiently, never pushing for more than I could give, never trying to plug the hole my mother had left with meaningless chatter.

But remaking your family when it's split into two parts is very hard, of course. We—my brothers and our various partners at various stages—would traipse to our mother's apartment at holidays when necessary. She got a boyfriend who quickly moved in just about a year after I moved out, and he stayed for the rest of her life. He was also an alcoholic, also divorced, also with growing children on their own. My feelings about him changed over the years, starting with blame and cold distance before finally landing on a kind of sympathy and thankfulness that my mother wasn't alone in the world in the last years of her life.

And we'd spend time with our father and his family, re-imagining ourselves now without my mother in the mix, even though she was still very much alive. We talked around her a lot then, because often there was nothing to say that wasn't painful or worrisome.

And then, when I met Josh and encountered his very different family, one where his parents were still happily married, where family holidays were loud and boisterous but not ever filled with fears that someone might get too drunk or leave in anger, I slowly tried to eke out a place among them, too.

Having Zelda brought us to a different place. Suddenly, there was something to talk about that wasn't superficial; we all had something in common. Something to focus on. Someone we all loved completely. I came to motherhood motherless and found that my daughter repaired bonds all over my life. She enabled me to open myself to a new place of honesty with my parents (my father, my stepmother) and with Josh's. I took less shit from people, I responded faster and with a shorter temper to unwanted tips on parenting, but I also found that I felt much closer to the family that I had.

It's an odd flipping of roles, to become a parent as your own parent watches. To see them fill their place as grandparents and to appreciate them in a new light. To watch that occur seamlessly, because it is a natural life transition, heals a lot of whatever has happened in the past to make you question how you feel about those closest to you. I never had outright rifts with people in my family, or my in-laws, mostly because I didn't bother arguing if something came up that I disagreed with. That changed once Zelda was around. My openness meant a new fire lit within me that made me louder and more self-assured, but it also meant a true, actual appreciation for my family.

It is strange, as a daughter, to see your father in a different light as a grandfather. When I was little, my father would sometimes sit silently at the kitchen table for easily two hours, petting our cat as she purred. I marveled then at the patience, and only when I became a mother to Zelda did I see that ability appear in myself. Only then, when my dad came to visit and held the sleeping newborn for hours so that I could eat or take a shower, did I see what all that quiet, stubborn kind of stillness could be worth.

The relationship that needed the most repairing, the one that I had with my mother, was more or less firmly in the past. Whatever changes would come to that would be internal: I'd "make peace" with her where I could, as if peace were possible. But Zelda's existence has seeped into all of us, her personality rolling over small slights or perceived ills as if they were nothing at all.

It's an overstatement to say that when a child arrives, healing follows. It's an overstatement of who I am to say that her mere existence brought me closer to my family. And yet it's at least partly true, at least part of the time. In simple terms, it's meant a greater effort on my part, to update and to spend holidays and extra time with my family and with Josh's. Proximity is stressful. But I've found it's also meaningful. And in that space, if I haven't exactly learned to feel okay with what came before, well, I've at least tried to accept it.

CHAPTER 15

. . .

My grandma Elly had a bit of dementia in her old age, so by the time I was nearing thirty, she often returned, when I visited her, to the same stories over and over. She'd always been a great storyteller, and I, like my mother before me, took great pleasure in talking to her for hours when I could. One of the things she remarked on for years and years was how when I was little, maybe only ten or eleven, I once told her that when I grew up I was going to move to New York and become a writer. I used to feel annoyance at my grandmother when she brought this up, not simply because it hadn't happened yet, but also because I didn't remember ever saying it. But once when she said it, I asked her: "What did you think of that?"

My grandmother was still alive when I did finally move to New York, and she was one of just two people who were happy about my decision. The other person was my mother.

In May of 2005, I finished a master's degree in English literature at Carnegie Mellon. Like most of my education, I had done all right but not outstanding. I was working full time throughout and pressed for time to study and manage the tendrils of my life effectively. I still had money concerns and was borrowing a lot just to go to school. When I finished that May, I didn't know what I was going to do next.

I started a band on a whim with three other women I barely knew at all, cobbled them together from friends of friends. All the men I knew at the time were in bands; my brother and my boyfriend Patrick were in the same band together. I'd been dating Patrick on and off for years. We'd lived together for part of my college career, then broken up at my request and I'd moved to a place of my own for a while, but we'd recently gotten back together while I was in graduate school. Patrick had gone to high school with me, and all his friends were my friends. He knew my family very well, and I knew his.

I was happy in the band for the months that I was in it. Applying myself to something like that, to writing songs and playing shows in a group of people, was very different than anything I'd ever done before, but like when I was at school, I didn't worry too much about where it was leading, didn't think of it in terms of the future, but tried to focus very much on what was right in front of my face. These girls made up a new set of friends for me, and at that point I was distanced from Emily, Vanessa, and Ellen. Emily had finished college and bought a house in a suburb near where we'd grown up. She was the most obviously successful of the four of us. Ellen had lived out west for years while we were all in college and then returned around the time I was applying to graduate school. She had a son and for a long time seemed happy with her husband and baby and new life. But I worried about her a lot already, from a distance. Anytime I'd seen her over the past few years, she almost always drank to incoherence, not remembering whatever had happened the following day. My band played a show once at the bar she owned with her husband, and she was drunk before we went on. I didn't judge her, but the sense that she was drifting out of control nagged at the back of my mind. Vanessa had married when we were just about nineteen years old and had a beautiful daughter. She moved to San Francisco and divorced, raising her daughter with her ex-husband cordially and successfully. She went back to school and started to build her own career and life, and from afar I was happy for her. None of us had any falling-out, but we were each on our own little path.

I think the girls in the band were closer with one another than they were with me, though they never complained to me when I declined to hang out with them in our spare time. We practiced three times a week and played shows most weekends, so that was enough socializing for me.

And then I met someone else.

In the summer of 2005, my brother and my boyfriend's band went to Brooklyn to record an album with Josh and his brother, Eric, who had built a recording studio in their apartment building. Josh and Eric were from Pittsburgh too, and my high school boyfriend Nick had met them going to raves in the 1990s when Josh was a DJ.

Sometime in July of that summer, Josh and Eric came home to go to the show my brother's band was having to celebrate the release of the album, and that's when I met Josh. It's hard to describe how I felt about him, a six-foot-four lanky guy who was loud and rude to me as I wandered around the after-party, but I sensed more than anything some kind of danger. Josh was complaining the entire party about his girlfriend, who had driven to Pittsburgh to meet him for the party and then dumped him and gone straight back home. I didn't know anyone like him. He was forceful and almost obnoxious but refreshing, because all my friends were very much like me, bottled up and awkward, never coming out and simply saying what was on their minds. To describe Josh as having no filter would be a real understatement, and though I barely knew him, I felt attracted to him and wanted to be near him. More than anything I wanted to just spend my entire night talking to him. About anything.

Which I did. And it did not go unnoticed. Though no one—not my boyfriend, my brother, or the other girls in my band, who were at the party and definitely witnessed me flirting—said anything to me, I felt almost immediately a divide come between me and all the friends I had in Pittsburgh.

And so by the time he came back to Pittsburgh for a holiday, maybe a month and a half later, I knew that I wanted to see him again. I found out by chance that he was in town; someone mentioned it casually: "Josh is here. He's DJing at a rave tonight," and I decided to find a way to go. A small group of us drove there: Josh, his friend Lenny, the drummer in my band, who was also named Laura, and me.

I hated raves, but I didn't really care. I just wanted to talk to Josh, and I think all the people we were with sensed it. I didn't care about that, either. The rave was, fittingly, at an old, abandoned roller-skating rink, huge and dark, the disco ball still hanging from the ceiling, and Josh lost his keys in the middle of it. They fell out of his pocket, and he showed me, for the first time, what I came to learn was a very classic Josh-style freak-out. He was yelling and wandering around, talking about how he was screwed, that he'd never find the keys. I wanted him to be calm, I told him we could find them, but he wouldn't listen.

So I wandered off on my own, cursing my horrible eyesight, as I silently poured over the floor for his keys. I found them in about two minutes, picked them up, walked over, and handed them to him. He hugged me and laughed and looked at me and said, "You're amazing."

I honestly don't know what the fuck I thought I was doing. I wasn't a great girlfriend, but I also didn't really openly lie to or cheat on people. I don't think I had ever encountered someone who I just felt compelled to pursue regardless of the consequences. And so, for the time, I didn't think of them at all. I simply went about my business, with my job and my band and my boyfriend, while at night, alone, I thought endlessly about Josh.

I lived divided, as I pursued long-distance my connection to Josh. I emailed with him and then later texted him, and finally we started to talk on the phone late at night, when I'd worked all day and was tired from band practice. I'd fall asleep listening to him talk a lot of the time, as though he'd replaced the radio shows I often listened to.

Josh and I left no air space between us from the moment I met him. Instead of feeling pressed to perform in a conversation, there was suddenly a person I just wanted to tell everything to. He was almost completely disconnected from my entire circle of acquaintance, most of whom I'd known since I was a child. Because I'd lived on my own through college and graduate school rather than in a dorm or a shared house, I'd never been thrown by circumstance into a new group of people. I'd gone through all of school without making any friends who stuck around beyond a certain class or semester.

Josh was a wholly new person, and I felt drawn to narrate my whole life to him, in a way that had never really been necessary before, because I so rarely encountered new people who wanted to know more than bits and pieces.

And though he was first and foremost a great talker, he was also a real listener; he listened and interjected his thoughts better than anyone I'd ever met.

In the end of October of that year, I decided to go and visit Josh for the weekend. I left straight from work on a Friday afternoon, expecting to come home on Sunday. I lied to everyone and told them I was going to New York with a friend from work. In the preceding weeks I had, in some cowardly fashion, tried to begin a slow and arduous process of breaking up with my boyfriend, but I felt so guilty and was so bad about doing it that I simply gave up and said nothing. He suspected I was lying to him but didn't say much. And instead of coming home that Sunday, I stayed with Josh until Tuesday or Wednesday, calling out of work and band practice, sitting around his place while he recorded a band and hanging out with him at night.

Two nights after I got home, he asked me to move to Brooklyn, and although I barely knew him and would have to leave everything that I knew behind, I said yes.

I quickly began to attack the process of telling everyone that I knew I was leaving to move in with someone they didn't even know I'd been talking to. I told my brother John and my boyfriend first. They were not happy. I called my father, who clearly thought I was crazy and who suggested I wait it out a bit to be sure. I was obstinate and one-tracked; I didn't care what anyone thought. I'd made up my mind and was leaving. I told the girls in my band and the rest of my friends.

I quit my job. I quit everything and told my landlord I was leaving. And then I left. I took very little with me, packed it into a truck that Josh drove to Brooklyn the day before I left in my car, with my dog Sal.

Almost no one was happy I was leaving. Everyone, I daresay, thought I was insane. My father, my brothers, and my friends all seemed to think that I would be back in defeat, that my relationship, which was so very new, wouldn't make it and that I would find that I'd quit everything to no end. Only my mother said, "Good for you." I called her when I was already on my way, driving from Pittsburgh to New York in the snow. I don't know why I called her on my way, but I was glad that I did. It was early afternoon, and she'd been drinking, but not so much that I couldn't hold down a conversation with her.

"I met someone, and I'm moving to New York, to Brooklyn," I said to her. I didn't ask her to come visit because I knew that she never would.

"I'm glad," she said, and she sounded so overwhelmingly happy for me.

"Everybody thinks I'm making a mistake," I said.

"Everybody is wrong most of the time," she said.

"I'm not coming back," I said.

"I know that. You've always done what you said you were going to do," she said.

That was the last time I ever talked to my mother.

The fact that Josh and I are still together ten years later probably speaks in my favor: I made the right decision. But at the time, even once I got to New York and made new friends slowly and looked for a job, I felt as though everyone back home hated me and was unhappy about what I was doing. There I was, reaching for a new start on every level, and feeling judged and defeated by all the people I cared about, who I had worked very hard in the preceding years to build some foundational relationships with that were distinct from the mess my mother had made.

Josh and I got along bumpily from the start. We didn't know each other well and were suddenly living together in a (to be fair, very large) one-bedroom apartment. But the connection that I felt to him was not something that ever flagged, and every time he told me I should move out, that he hated me, and later, that we should get divorced, I dug in my heels and stared at him, waiting it out.

"You didn't leave," he said to me once, coming out of our room, as I sat on a high stool, smoking out the window and writing in my journal. "I'm never going to," I said.

Josh and I were temperamentally matched very well, and here again I am somewhat thankful for how I was raised. I am persistent in my belief that I can outlast his anger or his annoyance and can see through to the other side of it, to where he forgets he is mad at me and is resolved again to be happy. I am this way precisely because I have had to outlast others before, my mother mostly, who was, to be clear, far less deserving of my persistence than Josh was.

In hindsight, it's quite obvious why my mother was supportive of me in my decision to move to New York: she wasn't a part of my daily life, she was several steps removed from it, and so it didn't pain her the way it pained those closest to me. She didn't see that I was hurting people in the process, even though I told her on the phone that everyone was angry, mostly because I was being so terrible to my boyfriend, who everyone loved aggressively. But I think too that she saw my definitive breakaway, geographically and emotionally, as in some ways inevitable. Like my grandmother, my mother had been privy to my private thought process for most of my life. Some people want to stay near their family and those they love for their whole lives. Some do not. My mother knew very well that I was in the latter category. I like to think that she was proud of me from afar for following my instincts and for striking out truly on my own. But of course, I'm not sure.

CHAPTER 16

. ♦ .

All I have ever heard for my entire life is, "You look just like your mother." This truth, that I look "just like" my mother, followed me around when she was living and continues to do so now that she's dead. It has flagged only in years since Zelda was born, replaced by, "She looks just like you." These are truths, and they're also not the whole truth.

My mother and I looked "just like" each other despite the fact that she was tiny and I am slightly above average height; that she was blond-haired and blue-eyed, while I have dirty-brown hair (my stylist once described it as "the color of hair") and dark brownish, muddy-green eyes. But we did look alike. Our faces carry the genetic material to its most obvious conclusion.

Zelda's face is my own face as a child. I see it in every photo of her, in her face when she sleeps. I pull my own childhood photos out of the closet and stare at them, and they look so much like her. Though her brown hair is curly and mine is straight, it is the same color. Her eyes are deeper and darker than mine, but they're the same eyes. The same little nose sitting there on the same face.

One morning when Zelda was about eight months old, I went in to her room to wake her from her nap. I'd seen on the baby monitor that she was asleep thirty seconds earlier, when I'd left the kitchen to walk upstairs, but by the time I opened her door, she was already sitting up, looking through the bars of her crib at me.

I jumped almost physically, then pulled my phone from my back pocket to take a photo, which I immediately texted to my brother John. "OMG who does this look like?" I wrote in the message. "Holy shit, Kath!" he responded immediately.

That was the first but not last time I saw my mother in my daughter's face. It was so overwhelming and so distinct and different from what I normally saw when I looked at her, but I see these little hints of others peeking out from her all the time. Josh, Josh's mother, my brother Daniel all occasionally greet me as I look to her face for an answer to the question: Who are we now?

Looking so much like your mother is very hard when you don't always have the greatest things to say about her. I looked in the mirror for years and saw, instead of myself, my mother, with all the requisite things that that title—"mother"—meant to me. I saw her face as I aged from a teenager to a young adult. I saw her hangover face in my hangovers, the way we puffed up and our eyes didn't get bloodshot but watery. I saw myself growing a line between my eyebrows from my perpetual scowl, the same scowl she carried around with her. I've always blamed my scowl on my mother, so who did she blame hers on?

There is a large blank space where my mother should be from 1996, when I moved out of her house, to 2007, when she died. In that space I saw her maybe twenty or twenty-five times, always for an hour or two, never much longer. In that space, she barely aged, until the last few years, when her face had sort of collapsed and morphed into her father's face as he had aged. She looked worn-out but not old then, nothing that a few weeks of sobriety and a good moisturizer couldn't fix.

If I age the way my mother and her mother aged, I'll look moderately young until I'm about fifty, and then I'll slowly begin to morph into an indeterminate age. In March of 2015, when Zelda was barely able to walk yet, just past her first birthday, my grandma Peg died at the age of ninety-one. I hadn't seen her in about two years; we'd grown far, far apart in the time since my mother had died. She was increasingly bitter and mean, and going to visit her was never easy without the weird but kind buffer my grandfather and mother had created. Left to visit her alone, I barely did. But she was happy at our wedding, and she was always kind on the surface. Only when we were alone did she bring up everything bad that had ever happened to her, and so much of that was, in her view, my mother's doing. I took Zelda, who had never met her, with me to her funeral, and there in her casket, my grandmother didn't look any older to me than she had when I was a little girl.

Only when I was about thirty-five did I think of upgrading my skin routine from Noxzema and Oil of Olay to something more aggressive, something more antiaging, and even now I am barely able to muster much energy beyond soap and water most nights before bed. I am resigned to the ravages of time; I accept them.

Now, when I look at myself, I see Zelda, not my mother.

I hope that when she looks in the mirror, she doesn't see me.

Zelda is a singular child, all her own, so I resist the urge sometimes to draw too many parallels between us. I want her to have her own identity, and so when just this morning, at a birthday party full of three-year-olds, two mothers walked up and introduced themselves, following with, "She is a picture of you!" I laughed this off as best as I could. We look alike. I looked like my own mother, I heard this all the time. Eventually, as I grew, I wanted for this not to be so for whatever reason.

She is her father, too. In that way, she is not like me: she is outgoing whereas I have too often lived inside my own head. I used to dream all day long simply of going to bed so that I could be alone with my thoughts. But I had three brothers, a full house; I never got to pick the shows on TV. Zelda has the whole space to herself: she is an only child and, at three years old, a determined one. She knows who she is and what she wants. I try simply to foster that, to give her good manners and a decent framework for moving forward.

My mother, either because she didn't have time or because the house burned down and took everything away, didn't leave me very much when she died.

What my mother did leave me with was her books. Not the actual copies: as I said, she left me almost nothing. I carried around in my mind her love of *Jane Eyre*. She'd taken her copy from her childhood home. I don't know what became of it. I sure looked for it there, in her third-floor apartment, after she died, but I couldn't find it. I collected my own copies, buying them new and old. She preferred Charlotte to Emily, and I doubt that she knew about Anne. When, at the age of twenty, I went to northern England and visited the home where the Brontës had lived and written their books, I sent my mother, who would still be alive for another seven years, a postcard. Before I'd left, my mother had visited me and given me a notebook to write in on my trip. "I'm so happy that you're going to finally travel. I love you," she wrote inside. I took the journal; I filled up its pages on my trip. I have that book. It's out in the garage right now, boxed up with the rest of my notebooks from college. My mother gave me *Jane Eyre*.

Most of what we are given by our parents isn't physical but a matter of proximity. My mother never sat me down and said, "Here, read these." I learned by her example. She sat on the couch at night watching TV, sewing, or reading a book, and I followed in her footsteps. She never told me to drink or not drink alcohol: I learned not to drink by watching her drink, and later, I learned to avoid thinking about it when I drank too much also from her example.

I have taken the best things from my mother that I could. I try not to waste time, as I can only feel that she wasted time. I hope to do better than my own mother did at mothering, which, after all, wasn't that bad anyway. She left no physical messes behind; I didn't have to spend weeks purging boxes of junk or donating piles of clothes to Goodwill. I should try to be thankful for that, though I know that I would give a lot to have a box or two from her like the ones I'm accumulating in my own garage. Again, I'm trying to right her wrongs, and so my daughter will have quite a task on her hands when I am gone. When I walk into the garage and see the boxes stacking up, in need of organizing or restacking, this is what I tell myself: Zelda will want these, probably.

My mother didn't leave me much, but she also left me everything that she had. What more could I ask for?

CHAPTER 17

• • •

When I started doing my family tree around 2005, I asked my grandma Peg about her father, who had died when she was eight years old. I asked her about him because I wanted to know how he died, at the age of thirty-eight. I suspected, of course, that he'd been an alcoholic. Peg never drank much, but as I grew up, I noticed that she herself carried some of the traits of a person who had been raised by an alcoholic. Even though he had died when she was so young, I knew from experience how quickly having a drinker for a parent could affect behavior. She kept secrets and worried so much about appearances. She talked about him with reverence and told me his appendix had burst, killing him.

But I did my own digging and found that, in fact, her father had died at thirty-eight because he drank too much. It was right there on his death certificate, which I requested from the Pennsylvania State archives. "Contributory factors: alcohol." I was in my late twenties by then, and many mysterious pieces of my grandmother's behavior over the years fell into place.

It is often comforting to focus your attention on the past

for confirmation of what you have yourself experienced. To find that in some ways we are all the sum of our pasts, to find connections from generation to generation. Alcoholism's genetics are poorly understood, but one thing is certain: the behavior is passed on.

I would love to say that my mother's alcoholism ended with her. That I got away clean, that drinking was never a problem for me. I would love to tell you that I was firmly dedicated to sobriety or that I was a fine social drinker who never had any problems of my own when it came to wine, beer, and everything in between. But it's a lot more complicated than that.

In hindsight, I guess, I never really met a drink of alcohol that I didn't love. My first tastes of alcohol—thinking about them—can still sort of make my spine feel funny and my belly get warm. Beer was the first booze I ever encountered, when I was maybe nine or ten, a stolen can shared among four or five friends. It was warm, and that warmth flowed into my body and covered me, softened me on the inside.

But only in high school did I really begin to actually drink. And we drank a lot. We drank only on the weekends (and Wednesdays), but that was the entire goal of Friday and Saturday, as I remember it. And inside, I think I suspected that I had something in common with my mother. I'd watched her drink and change and react to drinking enough to be sensitive to the signs of problems in others, and I wasn't blind to them in myself, either. I simply pretended not to see them in me. People often say that alcoholics lie to themselves more than anyone else. For me, that was untrue; I looked in the mirror and I was pretty brutally honest with myself: I knew from way early on that if I continued to drink, I would almost certainly have problems. It wasn't me I lied to or hid things from. It was everybody else.

The reason was simple: I needed one single point of escape from my mother and what she had done to me. My mother had made me overly anxious and worrisome. This is really common in children of alcoholics, because we can't depend on our parents, the one thing that should be crucially stable in life. And if I couldn't count on my mother to pick me up or be there when I needed her, what was there to not be anxious about? I always expected the rug to be pulled from beneath my feet. I worried over tiny details of schedules and timing and yet often avoided doing the work I needed to do for school or life simply because I was busy worrying, and worrying all the time is an exhausting, full-time job. It is not something you can do while keeping on top of everything else, even in a teenager's life.

I started smoking and drinking because everyone else around me did those things; they are, or were, normal at that time for suburban kids to try out. Because it was the '90s and all cool teenagers smoked and drank. I tried other drugs—I smoked weed and drank too much coffee or cough syrup—but I only really attached myself to booze and cigarettes. They went together very well, and they gave me peace of mind. After a drink or two, my mind slowed down. My heart beat slower. My blood pressure fell. I didn't feel anxious. And my personality—my real one, not the nervous worrier who took over my body most of the time—even began to make itself known sometimes.

I want to tell you that my true self is sober. But in some ways, my true me, the one who wasn't raised by an alcoholic, the one who is laid-back and cool, is the one who emerges after two or three—but not more—beers or glasses of wine. I open up, or flower outward. I am at ease. But knowing that I sometimes have trouble stopping at two or three has often stopped me from taking one drink.

Being a teenager is a weird hell for everyone, I'm sure. For me, it was an odd combination of hell and, well, not hell. I had begun to feel on the verge of autonomy: probably because I was actually on the verge of it. I could see the light at the end of this particular parent-driven tunnel. I'd started to see that it was okay to not worry every moment about my mother, that I could not control the situations around me. I'd begun to feel at home in my own body. I felt like myself sometimes, and if I didn't exactly love who that was, I could live with it.

But I couldn't escape my conditioning. Well, unless I drank, I soon realized. I beat myself up over this plenty.

As I said, I couldn't lie to myself. I knew what alcohol was, better than most kids my age, and I knew that I was playing with something really dangerous, something that, by design, got out of people's control all the time. If my mother, a strong adult person, couldn't change her behavior or control herself or keep it together for her kids, how could I?

Much to my surprise, though, I soon found out that I *could*—at least sort of—control myself. I began, right there in high school with my first forays into drinking, a pattern that would carry me all through college and graduate school and then into adulthood. When it mattered, when I needed to not drink, I never, ever drank. Sometimes, that meant abstaining for weeks or months. I could stop whenever I wanted to—ha!—and then bide my time, waiting until it made sense to begin drinking again. I did this over and over. For several years in college I maintained a strict "only on Fridays" rule about drinking. I was paying for college myself and working full time. I didn't want to blow those things; I was determined not to. So I made rules for myself.

How much damage can one person do drinking one night a week? Well, in my case, not very much.

At the beginning, drinking alcohol freed up my mind to think beyond the confines of my family's house, my family's problems, my family. I began to envision, truly for the first time since childhood, the possibilities of a life lived however I wanted. Alcohol, really, had something to do with that opening vista, and no matter how much I sort of wish that weren't the case, it definitely is.

How many drinkers quit? All of them quit almost every day, I guess. The thing about quitting is that you can quit even for fifteen minutes and really mean it. You can really mean it only until you don't, and even if you give up after those fifteen minutes, nothing takes that fifteen minutes from you: they're yours.

Our culture supports alcoholism in insidious, even well-meaning ways: we assume, by default, that whoever we are drinking with drinks, too. Nondrinkers aren't shunned, but they're not exactly fun to be around. I have been the one person not drinking as often as I have been one of the people who is. I am comfortable in both roles.

I didn't often drink, but when I did, it felt *too good*. When I did, I thought always of my mother, scared that I would somehow devolve, unwittingly, to the place where she had ended up, drinking secretly or at night when the kids were asleep. Barely ever even trying to quit, as far as I could tell.

The few times I suggested, to friends or men that I was dating, that maybe I should stop drinking, I was usually laughed off. Drunks are like . . . Charles Bukowski. My mother. It's obvious when someone has a problem. Wasn't it obvious that my mother did? They were right; they had a point. And yet, inside, I still wondered what fire I was playing with when I drank.

One night in graduate school in 2004, when I was twenty-five, I spent a night out with the other students, most of whom were a little younger than I was. I had a full-time job; I was the only person in my English lit class who did. I had my own, permanent apartment with cats and pots and pans. Pretty much everyone else was an out-of-towner—basically kids. We went out to a few bars, drinking as we went, taking a bus back to the part of town where my car was near midnight. I didn't want to drive, so a few of us went to a diner and sat there, talking and smoking (you could still smoke in restaurants in Pittsburgh then) for a few hours. By the time I walked out of the diner and back to my car, it was almost 3:00 in the morning. I was stone sober, at least in my mind.

And then I got pulled over two minutes later, music blasting from my car stereo, because one of my taillights was out. I was five minutes from home. I laughed off the walking sobriety test. When they asked if they could look in my trunk, I said, "Oh sure. It's a mess in there; I'm sorry." And when they asked if there were any needles in my car, I said, "What? What kind of needles?" It was my first police experience. I was far too dumb to even realize that I was already three-quarters of the way to being arrested.

The cop, who was extremely nice to me, told me that they would like to take me to a police station to have an actual sobriety test: to blow into a machine. "You can refuse," he said, "but that means we'll arrest you. If you go with us and willingly take the test, you can go back to your car if you pass. It's your choice," he added.

"This does not sound like much of a choice." I laughed, grabbing my purse and getting into the back of the police car.

At the police station, I blew a 0.02. This was nothing by legal standards. Pennsylvania's limit for alcohol and driving is 0.08. And yet, the officer informed me that Pennsylvania was a "zero tolerance" state, something he had failed to mention earlier: if you were pulled over for any legitimate reason, *any* alcohol in your blood was subject to penalties.

And so, at 4:30 in the morning on a Saturday night, I was hauled to Allegheny County Jail. They photographed me—I remember the cop who took my photo telling me that usually people didn't smile for their mug shots—and I was happy to oblige. I just rattled along, because all of this seemed so silly to me, and I assumed that I would be out in two or three hours; that's how they'd made it sound.

They threw me into a holding cell that was full of probably a dozen women, most of whose faces I remember—they're burned into me. They were there mostly for drugs and prostitution. "Why are you here?" a girl who seemed only half awake asked me from her place laying on the floor.

Another girl from the corner yelled, "A white girl! You *know* she's a DUI." She was right, I agreed. A white girl with a DUI. What a cliché.

And I didn't leave in two or three hours. I stayed long enough for three meals. I stayed long enough that the next morning came. They told us a judge would be there soon, and then she or he failed to appear. There was a Steelers game; judges were mysteriously hard to come by. Eventually, I was able to call and leave a message for my boyfriend, but I didn't know if he'd get the message, and I didn't know when I'd be out anyway. I stayed in jail for almost a whole day because of a Steelers game. We could hear the cops on duty screaming as the Steelers won, and another woman, who had clearly been there under similar circumstances before, stood up and said, "Fucking finally, we can get our judge."

I was shackled to the other girls, pulled through a series of long hallways that led us from the jail to the courthouse, where in thirty seconds a judge told me I needed to come back in two months to hear my fate. My fate was that nothing happened. I had to pay an $800 fine. My crimes didn't mean a loss of my license or even community service.

I'd like to say that this experience led me to stop drinking, but it didn't. I simply never drank and got behind the wheel of a car again. And I will never, ever forget what was scratched on the wall in a Sharpie marker of that holding cell. It read, simply, "Punck Ass Bicth."

◆　◆　◆

I want to tell you that I stopped drinking in January of 2007, after my mother died. And I did! I had quit smoking the year before and had weaned myself fully from drinking a few months before she died. This was lucky. I needed clarity in that time, and her death certainly made the matter of drinking clear to me. It was something I could not do.

But I slid back before the year was out, and drank, for instance, in the weeks leading up to our wedding in October of 2007. I did this mainly because it was easy. I'd never met less of a problem drinker than Josh. I've seen him actually drunk just a few times in a decade of knowing him, and though he's certainly seen me drunk more often, it wasn't devastatingly obvious to anyone—not even to him—that I should quit. This is a personal decision unless you are so clearly a drunk that your life has become damaging to others.

And New York City is a drinker's paradise. It's not just that there are bars everywhere, but that you never need to drive. There are cabs and sidewalks, which opens the possibilities for drinking more often a lot easier.

Josh and I were never partiers or even people who went out very much. When I drank, it was usually at home, in the late evening, until bedtime. It's hard to do damage that way. His moderation kept me safe in many ways.

I would like to tell you that I quit drinking in January of 2012, when Ellen died from alcoholism at the age of thirty-four, almost exactly five years after my mother.

In fact, my memories of Ellen's death and the days after it are foggy because we drank so much. After Emily called me in tears to tell me that she had died, we had a long conversation where the question "How does a thirty-four-year-old woman with a ten-year-old son die from drinking too much?" remained unanswered. I flew back to Pittsburgh a few days later. I took a week off work and traveled, for the first time in many years, alone, back home.

I had two drinks on the plane, staring out the window the whole time. And when I got there, Emily picked me up, and we went back to her house and sat at her dining room table. She'd bought a house of her own a few years earlier. She was single just then, right out of a long relationship that ended badly. We smoked and drank wine—just two bottles, but then three—and went to bed late, knowing the funeral the next morning would be bad.

And it was. What to say about a woman I hadn't seen in

four or five years? That I stopped talking to her because she drank too much was both true and untrue. Yeah, the last few times I'd seen her had been upsetting because she drank so much, but again, it wasn't that simple. I didn't excise her from my life; she just sort of faded. I'd been in contact with her more recently, as everyone I had ever known began to stream onto Facebook, but mostly we'd been happily, acceptingly distant for years.

She'd already been cremated. Her parents, who I hadn't seen in years, were there. Her mother was fighting cancer and was dead a year later herself. I didn't have any takeaways other than simple sadness. There was nothing to learn except that this couldn't happen to me. I couldn't let it; I *wouldn't* let it.

I want to tell you that I didn't drink after Zelda was born. But that's not true, either, because I did. Alcohol wasn't on my mind for several months after her birth; I was too tired. But slowly, I saw exactly *why* it was that so many of the new mothers around me talked really excitedly about their after-bedtime drinks. Relaxation. Time to yourself. Why not fill it with a little wine?

I never really drank around Zelda. I was too nervous; my rules wouldn't allow for it. But I started to drink sometimes after she went to bed. And then, for the first time in my adult life, it became an almost nightly habit. It crept up on me slowly. It was just a few drinks, two or three, a bottle of wine every couple of days. Nothing bad happened, just a woman relaxing with her wine. The image of the "wine mom" exists for a reason: society condones, even encourages this image and the behavior.

No one tells you how unfair it all feels. It's unfair that you can't enjoy something as simple as a calming glass of wine at the end of the day like pretty much every other person on the planet does, because your history or whatever makes you *you* is a problem.

I don't know if I couldn't enjoy it because of guilt or because I really had a problem. I don't know if it matters. What mattered was that I was always scared, despite continuing to head at the end of the day, pushing the stroller into the wine store, to pick up a few bottles for the week before taking my daughter home.

I was never drunk around Zelda. I never fell down carrying her or dropped her. I never missed a nap or a feeding or even snapped at her because I'd been drinking. I always waited until she went to bed, just like my mother.

But the reality of my life was this: Josh traveled a lot, and I did not. I was often home alone with my daughter for days at a time, and though I wasn't getting wasted, I began to have another worry: not that I would end up like my mother—though I still worried about that constantly—but that Zelda would wake up sick or an emergency would occur. Wouldn't an emergency situation be worse with two or three glasses of wine?

If I was honest with myself, and I have always tried to be honest in my questions of myself, even if I defer answering them for a while, I knew the answer was yes.

It wasn't finally a striking realization or a tragedy that made me stop. It was very simple: I didn't want to be someone who looked forward more to the part of the night after my daughter went to bed than the part when she was awake. It's hard to blame mothers for feeling that way, and I don't have any guilt about sighing with relief when I close her door at night, but I'd found that some days, I was already thinking about my pinot grigio while I was still reading Zelda her bedtime stories. There she was, enjoying the best part of her day, Mama standing beside her crib, and I was, at least sometimes, imagining myself into a Zelda-less future. A future with wine and cigarettes, which I had magically started smoking again at night.

Why did I have so many rules for myself about drinking? I couldn't just drink the way others did, that was why. I was always either *all in* or *all out*; I lived pulling the wagon behind me all the time, the wagon was always there. Why was there a wagon?

Did my mother go through this? There had been so few periods of sobriety for her that I knew of, and most of them had lasted weeks at a maximum, not months or years the way that I had managed. Did she have an internal struggle like I did, or was she unburdened by such doubts? I'd grown up feeling so disappointed in her, because she'd never even seemed to try. But I now wondered, what did she feel inside? Her struggle was struggled alone. I know it now.

But when I quit, it didn't matter what my mother had gone through. I was and am my own person. I didn't want to spend so much mental energy thinking about it anymore, and so for me, the easiest way seemed to be finally, fully, removing the possibility. Taking the option of drinking off the table was what I had to do. To cut myself off.

Which I did, in November of 2015. I snapped after Thanksgiving, moving into Christmas. I knew that holidays always resulted in at least one night where I drank a little too much from stress and then woke up unhappy to a full day's work, and I didn't want to do that ever again. So I decided not to.

I wanted to push back against inevitability. I wanted to stop ever worrying that someday I might trouble my daughter the way that I myself had been troubled by my mother. Zelda and I would argue, I knew, over things that mattered little and things that mattered very much.

But I could, right then, right now, push back against any inevitability of alcohol. I could make sure that never happened. I could see to it that my daughter never lived with the anxiety that I felt, never knowing for sure what version of Mom I would encounter when she picked—or didn't pick—me up from a school event or in the hallway outside my own bedroom late at night. The thought of her feeling that kind of worry on my behalf ached inside of me and pulled me into this new reality, where I felt alive and awake and solid.

I haven't had a hangover or even barely a headache in almost two years. I have rarely thought, "I'd like to have a drink," though there is some irreplaceable festivity created by a bottle of champagne that nothing, really, can replace—although I have found that IKEA Sparkling Pear Juice comes close. I feel less guilt, and I don't worry about my own health as much anymore. All I had to do was stop.

I hope against the future that I have, in this one way, bettered my mother in mothering.

CHAPTER 18

◆ ◆ ◆

I've always expressed myself better in writing than in words spoken out loud. And the first time I remember writing my mother a letter, I was still using crayons. In the boxes of stuff I took from her house after she died, there were a few handmade cards and drawings she'd saved over the years from my brothers and me, things that had survived the fire. And though I looked among her papers and in her drawers for the two letters I had written to her that weighed on my mind so heavily, I found only one of them.

I made her the card on a piece of blank white paper. Not construction paper, but copy paper. I remember the card very well, because I have it here, in my house. I don't know why she kept this, among the hundreds, maybe thousands of things I sent or made her in the twenty-nine years that I knew her. But I can guess.

The card was rudimentary, but not as rudimentary as my actual art skills (I am incredibly bad at drawing or really any visual art, always have been) because I copied the picture from a book. It was of a rabbit, the front half of its body there on the front of the card, the back half on the back side, around the bend from the fold. Inside the card read, "I love you mommy, thanks for everything you do for me." It was a ruse.

I left the card on my mother's dressing table in her room and didn't say a thing. Later, after she'd read it, I planned to pounce on her with my assessment of her life. Thinking of it right now, I feel nervous wonder at the balls it must have taken to confront her. The card was an apology, but in advance.

I don't remember exactly how it went down, though I feel embarrassment on behalf of both of us. I remember that I ended up calling her into my room, telling her I wanted to talk, which was quite common for us: the two women in a house of men, we often took refuge in my little quiet bedroom, closing the door against their noise. I don't remember what I said, but I can imagine it.

"Mom, we learned at school about alcoholics, and I think that's what you are. But it's treatable, there's a cure! I think you sometimes need to go to AA to fix it, but it can be better." It would have been something like this, so textbook and overly simple and still so true. So childlike and perfect. So very painful for me to think of even now.

My mother did what any cornered mother would do: she smiled and took it quietly. She assumed, incorrectly, that I was a lot dumber than I was. She assured me things would be different moving forward, that I didn't have to worry.

Parents think their kids want reassurances—"You don't have to worry." Maybe they do, when they're three or four. But by the time I was eight, nine, ten, I saw quite lucidly what was going on around me: I knew better than my parents. Somehow, in her walk from youth to adulthood, things had gotten all confused. My mother was wrong. She was wrong a lot. Every kid learns this about their parents eventually, that they can make mistakes; it's part of growing up. But some learn faster and harder than others.

The card that I will keep for the rest of my life makes something start to burn in my throat when I pull it out and examine it, not because of sadness but because of anger. Anger at myself for how smart but misguided I already was becoming.

Another characteristic of children of alcoholics, I've found, is that they'll always be better at pointing out and accurately assessing the problems of others than they are of themselves. They've usually had a lot of practice.

The second letter I wrote to my mother was in the beginning of November of 2006. I'd just gotten engaged to Josh and was living happily in Brooklyn. In fact, I was happier than I had ever been in my life, and I think that was the main reason that I decided to write to my mother, rather than call her. I wanted to keep the distance from her that I still needed, to protect and buffer myself against something unpleasant, but I also needed to share my happiness with her. At the time, I thought what I was doing was so adult, so different from the other times I'd confronted her. Now, I see the truth: I might as well have written the letter in crayon.

I have never really told anyone about the letter before; you are the first to know. It read more or less like this: "I am engaged to be married. I am happier than I have ever been. I want to help you go to rehab. I will do anything for you to make that happen, but if you don't, I want you to know that I will not invite you to my wedding." And then, I added, to my eternal horror, the following: "And if you don't stop, if you can't stop, and if I ever have children, you will never meet your grandchildren. I love you. Laura." I said more than this, of course. I pleaded with her; I told her how much I wanted her to be a part of my life. But the material facts are what they are. It was a letter that contained a bold statement of fact and a devastating threat.

I know why I wrote this letter. I was harsher to her in writing than I had ever been because I hoped, my last hope, to snap her out of it. I threatened her out of fear that she would never recover and out of a desperate need that she should. I threatened her with my happiness because I wanted her to be a part of it, but that happiness had come to me at a great price: I'd had to leave behind painful things, and the most painful loss was her.

I wanted my mother to hear me, to want to be with me, to love me. I wanted her to be proud of me, not just from afar but in my life with me. I wanted her to meet Josh and his family, to be a part of the suddenly wonderful life that we were having. My father had gotten engaged, too; he was going to get married in the spring, just a few months before Josh and me. I wanted her to have some chunk of the good things we were all slowly beginning to fill our time with.

I didn't know what her day-to-day life was like anymore. I don't know how she felt when she opened the mailbox and saw a letter from me. She was probably excited. I am filled with horror at the thought of her opening it, reading it alone, exhausted and disappointed.

I want to tell you that in these moments when I allow myself to think of the letter, I hate myself because I was the aggressor then. Instead of feeling victimized by my mother as

I had when I was a kid, I now must contend with the fact that in that last moment, in our last direct communication, she was the helpless one.

I understand why I wrote this letter. I would want nothing less than this from Zelda if I deserved it; it was on some level a symptom of my unfailing love for her, that I wrote it and said what I said. And yet, I live still with it as my truest regret. It is the worst thing I have ever done, and the fact that it contained nothing but the truth doesn't change that at all.

My mother never responded. Less than three months later, she was dead.

When we cleaned her apartment out after she died, I hoped that I would find that letter, partly out of a deep fear that it still existed, that someone else could read what I had written and judge me for what was, no doubt in my mind, my most regrettable action ever. Not because it wasn't true—all of it was blunt and true—but because it hadn't worked so it felt very pointless, with her dead and me still alive to lay awake at night in regret. I didn't find the letter. I hoped that she destroyed it.

Only after Zelda was alive, sitting at her desk with a pen one afternoon, so concentrated was she at that time on intently drawing tiny circles over and over, did I think of that letter in a new light. Though I still regretted it, though it stings me now to know that I wrote it, I looked at her and thought to myself, "I hope she loves me enough someday to say such dreadful things to me, if she must."

This is the only absolution I have allowed myself for that letter.

We didn't, in fact, clean out my mother's apartment right after she died, but several years later, when her partner died himself, from cancer. Before then, in the space where my mother was gone and he was still living, he stayed in their house and kept all my mother's things, her clothes, her papers, just as she had left them. Once he was gone and we were there, cleaning the place with Josh and my brothers, her boyfriend's son and wife, even my father was there, I found her makeup still in the bathroom cabinets.

My mother's boyfriend had said when my mother died that she had, at some point during her last year of living, sat down and written letters to each of us, her four kids. What on earth these letters could possibly say was a mystery. I envisioned, as we drove a small box truck to her apartment in anticipation of taking away whatever we were going to take with us, finding diaries, notebooks, papers stacked in the attic. I envisioned finding a letter addressed to me that might, somehow, unlock the mystery of who my mother was to me. Who she was beyond being the mother I had known and loved and fought with.

I imagined carting away notebooks and reading them, finding out the secrets of her life the way that anyone who dared dig among my own stash would discover the best and worst thoughts I've had in my years on this planet. The mundane observations, the lists of books I am reading, the to-do lists and the homework assignments—I've saved all of it. My father is a dedicated shredder of documents and paper. I am a pack rat. I thought my mother was more like me, so as I got closer to her home, I allowed myself to fantasize that I might find something of value, something that would help me make sense of everything.

But there was nothing. No letters, no diaries. I got her handwritten recipes, her address book from the 1980s, and a few scraps of things her kids had made her. I found a few pieces of paper that I walked away with as though they were gold simply because they had her distinctive, terrifically neat cursive handwriting on them. The cursive that she taught me, painstakingly, the year before I went to first grade.

My mother's secrets, if she had them, were never written down.

*   *   *

Every so often, I sit down at my desk, take out stationery, and write Zelda a letter. Sometimes, it's just a little "What's up, how are you?" Sometimes, I document new words or skills she has learned. Sometimes, I tell her things I would never say aloud. That I'm having a hard day. That I cried for no reason I could figure out. That I didn't want to get out of bed. I tell her these things in handwritten letters in the hope that she will want to read them. Even if she waits until she is fifty years old, I hope that someday these little missives have value for her.

I mail the letters from our house back to our house, so that they have postmarks, so that I can keep them in order in the shoebox I store them in. I do this partly because it appeals to me, partly because I want her to know how much I love her every step of the way, and partly because I wanted so much to have something written, something direct, something specific, from my own mother. I think this was part of the reason I began writing about her. I would have given almost anything to have insight into my own mother, to have known what she thought about me, but also more than me. To know anything and everything.

Someday, I hope Zelda knows that the many thousands of

ways I have exposed her person in my writing was all because she gave me the power, if not the permission, to do so. She made me, to a great extent, the writer and person that I am. I am thankful for that, and I hope that she is never too embarrassed of me for it. But I also want Zelda to know that my mother, her grandmother, made all this possible, too.

I am realistic about all of this. I know that where I am disappointed at how little my mother left me in writing, my own daughter is likely to be disappointed, or to not care about, how much I am giving to her. But she is her own person; she'll figure it out.

CHAPTER 19

⋆ ⋆ ⋆

On a Thursday at the end of January in 2007, at around 3:00 in the afternoon, I stood on the 7 train in my bulky wool winter coat. I'd been living in New York for less than a year by then, and it had been the happiest under-a-year of my adult life. I had a job that paid me well for not very much work. I loved my apartment. I was writing music again; I was thinking about going back to school. I'd left Pittsburgh in a rush, having just earned a master's degree but without having made any plans for what was next. After almost a year in a new place, I was finally thinking about what was next. The letter I had written to my mother had been weighing on me since I sent it, but most days my worries about it were momentary. I had had what I thought were good intentions in sending it, and it had done one—but only one—of the things I had hoped that it might, closing off a chapter for me. I felt as though I were moving on from my mother and that after years of avoiding her, I was now simply living without her.

Josh and I had been engaged for two months, and the engagement ring, as I stood there on the subway, still burned my finger a little bit, a constant presence that wasn't quite at home on my body yet. The subway was almost empty. It was not yet rush hour, and I think the city was still sleepy from the holidays that had recently ended.

I worked as an assistant to an executive at a commercial real estate firm. It was, as my coworker Maranda said, "the kind of job that is temporary forever." In fact, I had taken the job as a temp staffer through a temp firm. Probably half the admins at the company were temps, people who were paid fairly well—I think I made $20 an hour, which seemed like an enormous amount of money to me at the time—to have asses in seats. We answered phones; we managed calendars and wrote emails. Through the staffing agency, I wandered from job to job, most of them in Midtown, some on Wall Street. They were always admin or front desk jobs, usually lasting a week or a month. I was offered a full-time position within about a month of starting at the real estate place. I accepted because Josh, who was still producing music with his brother in the studio in our apartment building, didn't have a steady income and because our rent was cheap enough that this salary would mean we were more well off than I'd ever been.

I'd probably been working there for five months on that day in January when my brother Daniel called me. He called my cell phone, which was a Samsung flip phone I still have. This was well before the phone was glued to me at all times, and so I missed his first call, away from my desk for a coffee break with Maranda. I came back to my desk to a vibrating phone.

And here's where my fantastic memory fails me. I don't remember what my brother said to me. I remember, awkwardly, only that for the few minutes that the conversation went on, I was acutely aware of my surroundings. Jackie to my left, Maranda and Casey on my right, chattering away about something I couldn't make out. The artificial light seemed very harsh suddenly as I struggled to grasp the gist of what he was saying. Daniel never called me. I knew before I picked up that something was wrong.

The gist of what he said was this: come home, come quickly, something happened to Mom, and there isn't much time.

I didn't ask for details. I said okay and hung up the phone. I stood up and walked down the hall to the office of the HR manager. I told her I needed to leave, that something was wrong with my mother, and that I would let her know in the morning when I would be back.

I went back to my desk. I told Maranda and Jackie, who flocked around me. I think I said, "My mother is dying." I don't remember that either. I remember the shoes I was wearing. The skirt. I put on my coat and went into the bathroom and started to cry. I stopped myself. I left the bathroom and the building, stopping outside to smoke a cigarette before walking the few blocks up to Forty-Second Street, where I got the train.

As I stood there on the subway trying to get home to tell Josh that my mother was dying with my earbuds in my ears, pretending to listen to music but in reality listening to the train's mechanical hum, my eyes met the eyes of a stranger standing directly across from me. I realized then that I was visibly crying, tears just streaming down my face. I didn't typically cry in public. But I didn't care at all.

"Are you okay?" a kind-faced, chubby, middle-aged man standing across from me mouthed to me. I know he didn't say the words out loud because my iPod wasn't playing any music.

"No," I said, and as the word came out, so did a sort of low howl. It was the kind of sob I have only heard once or twice in my life. When I was in eighth grade, my grandfather died after being diagnosed with cancer just two months earlier. My father cried like that then. It sounded, I think in hindsight, like an animal dying. I didn't care. I continued to cry, and the man nodded at me as I got off at the next stop in Long Island City, left to walk alone across the Pulaski Bridge back home in silence.

I am ashamed, somehow, to remember that I considered not going anywhere; I considered staying home. My instinct told me to hunker down, to stay in New York where I was safe. I did not want to go back to Pittsburgh to face my dying mother.

"We have to go right now," Josh said. He wanted details. He wanted information I didn't have.

"What happened?" he probed me. I didn't know. I didn't want to ask too many questions. I didn't want to know. Was it not enough to know that she was in a coma? That she was on life support?

But we left an hour later, packing up my dog and some clothes. I remember packing clothes that I thought would be funeral appropriate, gray wool pants and a sweater. I smoked a cigarette out the window. I packed my journal. I didn't know that I wouldn't be able to write in it for the next two months.

And so a long, coffee-fueled car ride during which Josh and I did nothing but talk carried us back to Pittsburgh. I rambled on and on, telling him about my mother. It seemed so important suddenly, now that I realized he would probably never meet her. We got to his parents' house at 2:00 or 3:00 in the morning and collapsed for a few hours before heading to the hospital where my mother was. To her boyfriend, who couldn't speak, and to my two brothers (David wasn't there yet), my uncle, and my grandmother.

My mother's death certificate says that she died of liver failure. Though I know that when I arrived at the hospital I saw her before I saw the doctor who was treating her, I remember the doctor at the hospital better. He explained, and made a small, very bad drawing to go along with his explanation, that my mother's liver had stopped working. She had a coughing fit in her living room, spit up blood, and her heart stopped. Her boyfriend called 911. She was resuscitated. I don't know how long her heart was stopped. The doctor gave us no reason to hope that she was going to live. She couldn't breathe on her own. She wouldn't wake up. Her brain was damaged. Her organs were done for. It took me several minutes of listening to his explanation to realize that he was asking us—someone—to make a choice. The question of who exactly was her next of kin mattered greatly, all of a sudden.

We passed that day together. We sat there staring at her, sitting with her. I remember that, when my grandfather died back in 1989 when I was twelve years old, we spent what seemed like days pent up in the funeral home before the funeral actually happened, in a small stuffy room with his body. At one point, my three brothers, our two cousins, and I went outside and ran around the parking lot as though we were animals that had been set free from the zoo. I remember thinking then how out of joint time was: it was a weekday, I should be in school, but there I was, in a sad, other zone. A zone that mattered very much, where emotions, usually hidden, were on display. Where men cried and people let go of old grudges. Though I was an adult now, standing there staring at my not-very-old mother, rather than a middle schooler, I immediately got the same cooped-up, jittery feeling.

I hadn't seen my mother in two years or longer. The fact that I did not and do not remember the last time I saw her bothered me enough that I did not focus on it then, when I was seeing her. "What could it possibly matter now?" I thought.

Seeing someone in limbo is hard, especially if you haven't seen them in a long time. One tries—well, I did, anyway—to distinguish what parts of her looked different because she was dying and what parts because she had changed and aged since I'd last seen her.

And she had aged. I thought then, I think now, of Yossarian, in *Catch-22*: "Well, he died. You don't get any older than that." She looked as old as she was going to get. Ashen and colorless, bloodless.

The living want to live, and I felt acutely aware that my mother was in limbo: she wasn't going to live, but she wasn't dead yet. It felt wrong to leave her so that I could get coffee or a snack, and yet I desperately wanted diversion. I wanted to not be in that busy giant room in an ICU where other people were dying too, where the lights were always low because almost nobody there was ever going home. I wanted to run around in the parking lot.

That night, we went back to Josh's parents' house. I sat in the kitchen and talked to his mother, who, though she didn't know me well yet, was going to have something in common with me soon: she'd lost her mother when she was a young woman, too.

My mother was good at many things. She was always good in the crises that families inevitably go through. I felt acutely then the lack of her presence. No one really knew what to do. The fact that we all so desperately needed my mother when it was my mother who was dying is a true testament to the kind of family we were without her still. I called my father and talked to him for hours, more about the past than what to do in the present. The divorce had meant that, to a great extent, my brothers and I had to be the adults we were. My father didn't make decisions for my mother anymore, and I resented not him but the world, for a minute, for making it clear that as her only daughter, it was probably going to fall to me.

That's not accurate in any way, and I know it. But that was how it felt. It felt in those hours and days as if there was a spotlight shined directly at me and as if I was surrounded by hurt, defenseless people who needed my strength. Was this how my mother, the Decision Maker, had felt for years, surrounded by her family?

My grandmother was old and alone. Never mentally stable, she had sunken into a blackness I have never seen before. Because Josh had never met her or my mother previously, I still shudder to think that this was his first encounter with my mother's family. Peg replayed, in narratives we had all heard so many times before, the deaths of my grandfather and her brothers and sisters. Her father. She said at one point, "I'd have been just as happy if I'd never had kids." I had to witness my family through the eyes of someone else—Josh—who had to experience them at their worst, not their best.

My mother's partner of the past decade was a quiet and gentle person whom I did not know very well. I had, however, assumed the worst of him: Who could, after all, live happily with someone so clearly sick, so often not herself? So reduced from what I had known of her at her best? I felt at first puzzled by, then a deep respect and growing awareness for, his feelings for her. He was clearly devastated. It seemed he didn't view her as the broken and lost cause that I had for so long. I was overwhelmed with gratitude and with happiness to know that she was loved as she was, not as if she was some reduced version of herself. I couldn't accept her. But it made me happy that someone else could.

The next morning, I awoke clear on my purpose. Though I had quickly accepted the reality of the situation and had no doubt that my mother was done for, Josh convinced me that the smartest thing was to seek the opinion of a second doctor. There was some talk of what ifs, and though I don't think he intended to give me any false hopes, for a brief hour I imagined a scenario in which she recovered. Where she needed rehabilitation or twenty-four-hour care. Where she was different than she used to be. Where she didn't drink anymore, like my great-uncle, whose life was changed in a moment when he had a stroke. Maybe her old habits had died with this event. Maybe there was a chance.

I dressed myself and had coffee at 5:00 in the morning, sitting alone in the kitchen of my future husband's parents' home. A place that was happy for me. A place where I loved and felt safe. I knew that whatever was ahead of me, the day would be very long and very sad. I didn't feel like running through the parking lot anymore.

The second opinion came fast and hard; our hopes, such as they were, were tamped down quickly. The staff at the hospital must have been used to eleventh-hour delusions such as these, but in fairness to ourselves, asserting our needs and asks at that moment changed everything that happened thereafter. Now, it was clear: we were the ones to decide.

And that decision needed to be made. My mother had not made any arrangements for herself. This was not a surprise on any level: she had no savings, owned no real estate. She had nothing so valuable as to require insurance. So it made sense, of course, that she hadn't left any instructions about what we should do if she died. She was fifty-two years old.

My mother died within two hours of being removed from life support, which occurred after all of us agreed that we were ready to let that life take its course. There was not really any dissent, though her partner had a harder time accepting that this was really the end of her life. I admired his ability to hope in the circumstances. I felt jealous of his closeness to her in the final days of her life. I felt scared to ask about what had happened two days earlier.

She died on a Sunday evening. It was cold, and the trees were bare. The worst time of year in Pennsylvania. I told myself I'd be back in New York three days later. Then I would have time to face what had happened. Now I needed to plan. To make arrangements. To write an obituary.

At some point several hours before my mother died, a woman came to us and talked over what would happen to my mother's body when she died. She asked if we had a funeral home in mind; we did. She asked if we had known our mother's wishes regarding organ donation. I think I laughed aloud.

"I mean," I faltered, "is that an option for her? Is there anything worth donating?" I looked around me. Everyone understood what I meant: surely this body she was about to dispose of was useless to others, so recklessly had she abused it in the past years.

"Because of the nature of your mother's illness, her heart, kidneys, and liver are not donatable," the woman agreed. "But her eyes are."

Even today, I think about the fact that someone somewhere is walking around with one or both of her eyes (or parts of them, anyway: it's certainly more poetic to think of it as the entire eye). One of those same eyes that witnessed my birth, the birth of my three brothers. Eyes that witnessed all the things in her life that I didn't see. Eyes that were with her when I was not. It makes me feel something akin to happiness when I think that one or both of those eyes still see just now. Awake, like me, at 5:00 a.m. on a Sunday, one day after the tenth anniversary of her death.

I think too about all the things those eyes did not see. Her daughter getting married, her granddaughter being born. And I realize, when I think about her eyes and the fact that she was missing from those great events, the happiest parts of my life all lived after she was gone, that what I wrote to her in that letter just months before she died wasn't true at all. I wouldn't have kept Zelda from her. I just didn't know that then, before she was dead and before Zelda was born. And like my mother's boyfriend, I suspect it would never have occurred to Zelda to think of my mother as I did: as less than I wanted her to be.

I want to say that my mother dying wasn't a surprise, but it was. Even knowing what I knew about her, even knowing how hard on her body she had been, she'd always seemed immortal to me. But she wasn't, and her death was in many respects a relief to me. I don't mean that I was happy she was gone. I wasn't. But her death ended that slow, constant bubbling of worry that I had had for as long as I could remember and answered the question of what I was going to do about our relationship: it was over.

CHAPTER 20

◆　◆　◆

On a Wednesday in June of 1977, my mother, who was born on a Wednesday in August, gave birth to me, and I became her daughter. She was not quite twenty-five years old when I arrived, just four years after my brother David (who was born on a Tuesday in July). I was named after my father, Lawrence Joseph: Laura June. But I was also named after my mother, Kathleen June.

At the age of twenty-seven, I began to construct a family tree, partly because the bureaucratic, paper trail nature of genealogy appealed to me and partly because I wanted to trace the origin of my middle name, June. I knew that my mother, my grandmother, and my great-grandmother had all been given it by their mothers, but I wanted to find the beginning. I found that most of us Junes were born on Wednesdays.

When I started looking for Junes and building my family tree, I had no relationship with my mother to speak of. I actively avoided her calls, in fact, and a big part of me assumed that I would probably never have children. If I had thought about it further or been asked about it, I think I would have said that I would not give a daughter of mine the middle name June, even though I like the idea of a matrilineal name.

As I sat at my computer, or at the dining room table of our Brooklyn apartment, I didn't think I was looking for "meaning" in a grand sense. I wasn't drawing conclusions; I was looking for facts. I found them. Thousands of facts. The secret joy of doing something like a family tree is that the potential number of facts is infinite, and the work is never done. I hunkered down and drowned myself in the details. I forgot about my initial goal—looking for June #1—for months at a time, mired in the muck of searching for lost cousins or a dead and forgotten infant sibling of a long-dead aunt or uncle I had never met. I traveled back six or seven generations, and when the trail dried up, I moved onto constructing a family tree for my husband Josh, satisfied as I linked our trees together with our marriage. It was a warm but lonely place to be: obsessed with my distant origins while my actual relationships with my family were, to be blunt, not good.

"Oh June, because you were born in June," people have said to me my whole life. To which I have often said, "Well, my mother is a June and she was born in August." I'm nothing if not an arguer of minute technicalities that matter sometimes only to me.

"Oh," the people usually say, seeming deflated or confused, as if the answer isn't satisfactory. And it isn't, I agree. I've been looking for almost fifteen years now for a better answer, but I haven't found one yet. I don't know what the point is, and I suspect there isn't one. Just like everyone else with a family name, it's just a name passed down.

But when I knew that I was pregnant and that I was going

to have a girl, the middle name came to us first; there was barely a discussion of it. Josh and I agreed on that: whoever she was going to be, she would be [insert name] June. My mother was long gone. The name was something I liked so much, in fact, that I had taken to using it as my surname in my writing, partly to distinguish myself from my husband, who was also a writer, and partly because it just sounded so good. My mother always called me by my full name, Laura June. It's part of me, and now, it's part of Zelda, too. Carrying around that name draws a line between her and me; she's the latest link in the chain that reaches back across generations through the meaningless details and calls out to each of us, that we were cared for enough to be given a little piece of everything that preceded ourselves. I'm not a traditional person; I don't value heirlooms or get sentimental very often. But rather than think of the name as an albatross, I have decided to think of it as a distinction.

A few weeks ago, Zelda and I were driving back from a morning birthday party, with her strapped in her car seat in the back. It was about 12:30 p.m., and she usually naps at about 1:00 p.m., so I put on Lorde. "I don't want to sleep!" she wailed, because of course now she knows that Lorde playing quietly in the car means that it's nap time. The opening of *Pure Heroine* enrages her, but by track three or four, she's almost always passed out, her little head slumping over, her now long, thin legs dangling over the edge of her car seat. I don't know yet if she'll be tall like her dad or simply average like me, but she seems so large to me already. Only when she's asleep do the last vestiges of babyhood reveal themselves, her mouth an almost frowning O, her tiny hands balled into fists. She often sweats in her sleep like I do.

She quieted down as Lorde played, got lost in her own thoughts. We have our rules about what we do when we're driving around, and the goal is for Zelda to sleep. We don't make eye contact; we don't talk much, even if she asks a direct question.

Zelda stared out the window and was quiet. Her eyes were almost glazed over, and I thought she was on the road to Sleepy Town. But sometimes, in the weird space between awake and sleep, we are wont to have our most incisive thoughts. Three-and-a-half-year-olds, I have found out, are no different.

"You're not an orphan . . . ," she said bluntly, quietly, still looking out the window. "But . . . Nana isn't your mommy," she went on. Zelda is obsessed with orphans because of *Annie*, and Nana is my stepmother. "So . . . ," she went on, struggling to think. I could see her gears turning in the rearview mirror. "Who is your mama?"

Zelda doesn't know about death yet. She doesn't know that people are here and then gone forever. Her concept of "da life cycle," as she calls it, is that once we live long enough, we get to be babies again. I wanted to answer her truthfully, but in a way that wouldn't lead to further questions yet.

"Her name was Kathy," I said.

"That's a nice name," she said, still staring out the window. "I liked that birthday party." She moved on and hasn't brought it up again. One day, I'll be ready to tell her everything. I'll be ready to explain how much my mother would have loved her and how much she loved me. I'm not ready yet.

It's not easy to know people, to *really* know them. I've

worked very hard in the past three and a half years to parent, to mother, in a way that reveals my true self to Zelda without horrifying her too much. I want her to know more about me than I know about my own mother, and I feel like that's possible, because I have chosen not to carry secrets with me through life the way that I am certain my own mother did. Secrets can weigh us down. We are all entitled to our private selves, our private thoughts. Even babies, like my mother taught me thirty years ago. But if there is any value to making a chosen family, to my relationship with Josh, it is that he has enabled me to choose honesty, even if only just between ourselves. That alone freed me to begin.

I've been talking to myself since before I can remember, holding down a narrative of myself day to day, year to year. I always thought that maybe it was a special feature of just myself, but Zelda has led me to believe otherwise, that we humans are naturally bent toward self-narration. That telling stories about ourselves to ourselves is second nature, that it helps us to understand ourselves and our relationships with other people. Every night at bedtime now, as I said, she wants to hear about the story of her birth.

She wants to hear about when she was born, but she also wants to hear about the day before she was born: one day out of the many days she didn't exist yet. "I wasn't here then," she says. She's beginning to sense that her existence here hasn't always been.

"You were born on a Tuesday in February," I begin.

I have watched Zelda struggle to master the basics, walking and running and hopping on one foot. It reminds me that I once did the same, and that my mother too was just a toddling little girl, adored by her parents, not so long ago. But

I marvel to see my daughter working out, mentally and emotionally, a concept of time that doesn't have her as the center, realizing that there was a time before she existed. I see in her new body and mind a little piece of myself, laying in my bed at night decades ago, sucking my thumb, talking to myself, narrating my day to I wasn't sure whom. My memory is that I've always known I wasn't the center of my own story; my mother was. I've always believed that whatever it was I had to work out in life, somehow, she held the answer. But it's an answer I can't find, no matter how hard I struggle to make sense of my mother, her life, and how her story intertwined with mine. I still haven't figured it out, but in Zelda I have found that being the center of someone else's life is somewhat inevitable, if you are a mother. My daughter depends on me to tell her her story, to remember the things she loses to time. I hope I do it well.

ACKNOWLEDGMENTS

My gratitude and love belong to Joshua and Zelda June To-polsky, Valentina Caballero, Carmen Virginia Johns, Dr. Jacques Moritz, Jimmy Miller, Emily Chambers, Vanessa Blyth-Gaeta, Eric Topolsky, Katie Notopoulos, Silvia Killing-sworth, Andrew and Darla Childs, Katie Baker, Jen Gann, Paul Ford, Leah Finnegan, Lisa Klimkiewicz, and Maria Bustillos.

Thanks to my coworkers at *The Outline* and thanks to Andrew's Couch for the logs.

To the editors of *The Awl* and *The Cut*, who helped me to shape my first writings on motherhood—Alex Balk, Choire Sicha, Matt Buchanan, John Herrman, Stella Bugbee, and Izzy Grinspan: thank you.

My agent, Nicole Tourtelot, was the first person to help me begin to mold my work into something larger and louder and for that: thank you.

My editor at Penguin, Sarah Stein, has worked harder on my writing than anyone ever has, and has made it better than it's ever been in the process: thank you.

Also, to Shannon Kelly at Penguin: thank you for all of your help getting the book through its many, many revisions.

To Carmen Mader and Nicole Mayer, who I met and got to know while writing this, and who gave me something more pressing to think about than myself: thank you.

And finally, to my father, Larry, my brothers, David, Daniel, and John, my stepmother, Donna, and my mother- and father-in-law, Susan and Dave: thank you for your support and kindness and love.